FROM EARTH TO GLORY
COMFORTING THOUGHTS FROM PSALM 23

"MY CUP RUNS OVER!"

His love has no limit,
His grace has no measure,
His power has no boundary
  known unto men:
For out of His infinite riches in Jesus
He giveth, and giveth, and
  giveth again.

Annie Johnston Flint.

FROM EARTH TO GLORY

Comforting Thoughts from PSALM 23

DENIS LYLE

Christian Year Publications

ISBN-13: 978 1 872734 48 4

Copyright © 2017 by Denis Lyle

All rights reserved. No part of this publication may be reproduced, stored in a retrievable system, or transmitted in any form or by any other means – electronic, mechanical, photocopy, recording or otherwise – without prior permission of the copyright owner.

Typeset by John Ritchie Ltd., Kilmarnock
Printed by Bell & Bain Ltd., Glasgow

Contents

Foreword		9
Preface		13
Introduction		15
Chapter 1.	The Sufficiency Of The Lord	17
Chapter 2.	Success Over Stress	28
Chapter 3.	The Ministry Of Restoration	40
Chapter 4.	Victory In The Valley	51
Chapter 5.	How Good Is The God We Adore	62
Chapter 6.	It Is Good Now, But It Is Better Up Ahead	73

Foreword

King David's son, King Solomon, wrote, "A word fitly spoken is like apples of gold in pictures of silver." When he wrote this I wonder did he have in mind the lyrics that flowed from his father's pen. No words could be more appropriate than these to describe Psalm 23, the sweetest of songs penned by the Shepherd-King of Israel. In six short verses David left us a classic of literature, a masterpiece of genius and a well proved testimony of the relationship we, the sheep, may have with our great Shepherd, the Lord Jesus Christ.

This Psalm is sometimes referred to as "The Shepherd's Psalm", but in truth, it is David assuming the role of a sheep to speak of the contentment, confidence, company and contemplation it enjoys with its Shepherd.

In this book my good friend, Pastor Denis Lyle, explores and expounds the rich truths contained in the Psalm. His explanation of the text is faithful, his insights are helpful, his devotional thoughts are heart-warming, his copious illustrations are practical and the whole tenor of this work is Christ-exalting.

I whole-heartedly commend this book to you.

Victor Maxwell
President of Acre International
Lisburn
Northern Ireland

PSALM 23

¹ "The LORD is my shepherd; I shall not want.

² He maketh me to lie down in green pastures: He leadeth me beside the still waters.

³ He restoreth my soul: He leadeth me in the paths of righteousness for His name's sake.

⁴ Yea, though I walk through the valley of the shadow of death, I will fear no evil: for Thou art with me; Thy rod and Thy staff they comfort me.

⁵ Thou preparest a table before me in the presence of mine enemies: Thou anointest my head with oil; my cup runneth over.

⁶ Surely goodness and mercy shall follow me all the days of my life: and I will dwell in the house of the LORD for ever."

Preface

This book is the outcome of a series of studies conducted in Lurgan Baptist Church, Northern Ireland between March and May 2014.

During the series I drew widely from writers both old and new. Such books as:

1. "A Shepherd Looks at Psalm 23" by Phillip Keller
2. "The Lord is my Shepherd" by Robert Morgan
3. "The Lord is my Shepherd" by Clarence Sexton
4. "Holman Old Testament Commentary - Psalms 1-75" by Steven Lawson
5. "Exploring the Psalms" by John Phillips
6. "The Treasury of David" by C.H. Spurgeon
7. "The Lord is my Shepherd" by Dr. Adrian Rogers
8. "The Shepherd and His Sheep" by William Rogers

inspired me and helped me greatly. I have drawn widely from all of the above and no doubt many more. That is my disclaimer to plagiarism.

Denis Lyle
Lurgan Baptist Church
March 2017

Introduction

Think of Psalm 23 as a book of six chapters, with each verse being a chapter. Then, think of this Psalm as a book that describes the journey we are on. The journey of the Christian through life. Now, let us jump to the last chapter and when we take a peep at this last chapter we see that when this journey is over we will *"dwell in the house of the Lord for ever"*.

You see, we can entitle this book: **"From Earth to Glory"** for we, as believers, have the assurance that when this life is over and our journey is complete, we have a heavenly home awaiting us.

The story is told of the lady who found out she had cancer and that she had only about three months to live. She rang her pastor and asked him to come to her house so that they could arrange her funeral service. She told him what hymns she wanted sung, what verses from the Bible she wanted read, and then she said: "Pastor, I have one final request. You may think it strange, but I want to be buried with my Bible in one hand and a fork in my other hand". The pastor was somewhat taken aback by the request and asked: "If you don't mind, may I ask why you want to be buried with a fork in your hand?"

She replied: "Pastor, I know it is a strange request, but down through the years I have attended many suppers and banquets, and when the main course was eaten and they were clearing away the dishes, someone would say: 'Keep your fork.' I knew what they meant. The best was yet to come! Chocolate cake or apple pie or banana pudding. Pastor, when people walk by my casket, see the fork in my hand and ask: 'Why the fork?' I want you to tell them that the best is yet to come".

As believers, we know the best is yet to come. *"Goodness and mercy"* may follow us *"all the days of our lives"*, but the best is yet to come for *"I will dwell in the house of the Lord for ever"*.

Heaven is our final destination. But it is the journey, described in the first five verses of this Psalm, that we often struggle with. We can sing about *"the sweet by and by"*, but it is *"the nasty now and now"* that gives us trouble.

Getting there is settled and sure, but it is the going there that is rough. It is the journey that gives us trouble. Yet Psalm 23 tells us how to face the days ahead. There is *the day* ahead, when we get home, but until then, there are *the days* ahead. How do we face the days ahead? Well, I believe our beloved friend and companion, the 23rd Psalm, tells us how.

If a poll were taken of Christians, this Psalm would no doubt be the most popular portion of the Word of God. This Psalm has been a companion at the fireside, at the bedside and at the graveside. It consists of 118 words - only 55 in the original Hebrew - yet it sums up all our needs in life and all the abundance of God's grace.

It begins with *"the LORD"* and it ends with *"forever."* What could be better than that?

"The world could afford to spare many a magnificent library better than it could dispense with this little Psalm of six verses", observed William Evans, a writer of yesteryear.

Yes, it consists of 118 words, yet 116 are devoted to explaining the first two, *"The LORD."* You see, this Psalm is all about *"the LORD."* Here is how David faced life and in so doing he gives us the secret to facing the days ahead. What was David's secret? This man who wrote almost half of the Psalms, what was his secret? His secret was the Lord. David was captivated with the Lord. He was able to face life and all that life threw at him because of the Lord.

CHAPTER 1

The Sufficiency Of The Lord

We should notice right away:

(1) THE MAJESTY OF THE SOVEREIGN.

Do you see how David begins? "The LORD."

But who is the Lord? What is His character? Does He have adequate credentials to be my Shepherd?

We could take every word in that opening phrase and underline it. He is: "The LORD" and not: "A LORD". When David wrote this Psalm, the Egyptians had 365 primary gods - one for every day of the year. The Canaanites had many gods. But, David knew there was but one true God - the great, sovereign, eternal God.

"The LORD is." Many years ago, the great preacher S. M. Lockridge preached on the Lordship of Christ, and quoted this phrase: "The LORD is ...." He said: "The Lord always has been *is* and the Lord always will be *is*." He was stressing the eternality and the immutability of God. You just cannot keep the tenses straight when you think of our great God.

"The LORD is My" - not "the" or "a" but "my" Shepherd, the One who is responsible for every care the sheep might have. Yes, here we have the *Majesty of the Sovereign*.

Can you see: **(a) THE MAJESTY OF HIS NAME**?

"The LORD." The Hebrew word that David uses here would be

pronounced something like "Yahweh", which gives us the English rendering "Jehovah". Did you notice that it is in capitals? You see, God's name is almost always translated "LORD" in the English Bible. The reason it is like this is to tell us that it is a translation of an Old Testament name for God that is the most sacred name for Deity the Jews had. It is the word *"Jehovah"*.

According to Thomas Newberry, the name "Jehovah" combines the three tenses of the Hebrew verb: "to be" - "He will be" (the future); "being" (the present) and "He was" (the past). The name signifies God as the One "who is, who was, and who is to be", the eternal God.

"Jehovah is my Shepherd." That name was sacred to the Jewish people. So sacred that some Bible historians say that it was only pronounced once a year when the high priest would go into the "holy of holies", and whisper the name: "Jehovah". The Jews never spoke that name audibly and when a Jewish scribe was translating the Scripture, when he would come to the name "Jehovah", he would set down his pen and get a new pen just to write the name "Jehovah". The great, awesome, covenant-keeping God, the great *"I am."*

So, every time we hear the word "Yahweh", or "Jehovah", every time you see "LORD" in the English Bible, you should think: this is a proper name like "Peter" or "John", built out of the word for *"I am"* and it is reminding us each time that God absolutely *is*.

Do you remember when God appeared to another shepherd back in the book of Exodus? Moses asked God for His name? Do you recall the answer? "And God said unto Moses, I AM THAT I AM" (Exodus 3 verse 14). It just comes from the same root word as "Jehovah". "I am that I am." God - almighty, unchanging and unchangeable. "I am self-existing, self-existent, the Creator not the created. I was, and I am, and I will be, from everlasting to everlasting, First and Last, Beginning and End, Alpha and Omega."

Do you know what is missing from our lives? A contemplation

Chapter 1

of God! Do we not spend hours contemplating our problems, our family difficulties, our finances, our sport, and our holidays, but how much time do we give to contemplate the Lord?

C.H. Spurgeon opened his morning sermon on 7th January 1855 like this: "It has been said by someone that 'the proper study of mankind is man'. I will not oppose the idea, but I believe that it is equally true that proper study of God's elect is God. The proper study of a Christian is the Godhead. The highest science, the loftiest speculation, the mightiest philosophy which can ever engage the attention of a child of God is the name, the nature, the person, the work, the doings and the existence of the great God whom he calls his Father. There is something exceedingly improving to the mind in a contemplation of the divinity".

Contemplating God balances our thoughts, humbles our hearts, clarifies our perspectives, reassures our spirits and strengthens our souls. As we think rightly about God, everything else assumes proper perspective.

Then there is: *(b) **THE MAJESTY OF HIS NATURE.***

"The LORD *is*." That word *"is"* denotes existence. If something *is*, it exists. This is the tiny word that confounds the atheists. There it stands in all its naked force, the opening statement of the Psalm. No attempt is made to water it down, to apologise to a sceptical age, even to prove that God is. The Holy Spirit simply deems certain truths to be self-evident. The first and foremost of these - that the Lord *is*.

Do you believe in the existence of God? Do you believe in the reality of God? Psalm 23 verse 1: *"The Lord is"*. Genesis 1 verse 1: *"In the beginning God."* We live in a day when atheistic billboards and bus signs are found everywhere. They often say something like this: *"Millions are good without God"* or: *"In the beginning man created God"* or: *"There's probably no God."* A church in Johannesburg, South Africa, posted an opposing billboard. It showed a young man, deep in thought but with an empty head. Accompanying the image was a quote from the British poet Francis Thompson: *"An atheist is a man who believes himself to be an accident"*. That did not go down well with city officials and atheists, so they had it taken down. But we believe: "The Lord *is*".

How good to see the majesty of His name and the majesty of His nature – and *(c): THE MAJESTY OF HIS NEARNESS.*

For those two letters *"is"* not only indicate existence but immediacy. It is the present tense. The Psalmist does not say: "The LORD *was* my Shepherd", or: "The LORD *will be* my Shepherd", but: "The LORD *is* my Shepherd". He is my Shepherd presently. The Lord Jesus, though timeless and eternal, is now and He is accessible, a God of the moment and a God of every moment.

You see, what we have to realise is that the word *"is"* is not a promise - for a promise is a statement that declares what God is going to do in the future. In a wide variety of promises, the Lord tells us: *"I will do this"* or *"I will do that"*. These verbs are typically in future tense. The promises of God are His guarantees amidst life's uncertainties. But the opening verse of this Psalm is written in the present tense. It does not await fulfilment. It is not a prediction. It is a fact. This is not a promise to claim - this is a reality to experience.

Our Lord is a Shepherd whose presence is instant, immediate and accessible every day, every hour and every moment. *"The Lord is."* Jacob said: *"Surely the LORD is in this place; and I knew it not"* (Genesis 28 verse 16). Moses said: *"The eternal God is thy refuge, and underneath are the everlasting arms"* (Deuteronomy 33 verse 27). Paul said: *"God is faithful"* (1 Corinthians 1 verse 9) and David says: *"The LORD is my Shepherd"*.

What a way to open the Psalm! To get our focus on the Lord.

When you think about the journey of life, does it not give you courage to know that the omnipotent God is your Lord?

When you think about the days ahead, does it not give you strength to know that the omnipresent God is your Lord?

Chapter 1

When you think about the future, does it not give you hope to know that the omniscient God is your Lord?

How can we face the days ahead?

Well, don't look at the path.

Don't look at the problems.

Look at the Person.

Following the devastating 2010 earthquake in Haiti, a lady was buried beneath the rubble. It took several days for the rescuers to reach her. Do you know how she survived? By continuously quoting the 23rd Psalm.

Here is the most powerful opening for history's most precious poem. *"The LORD is ..."* He *is* here now for you and me. The Majesty of the Sovereign!

Then, still in this first verse:

(2) THE MINISTRY OF THE SHEPHERD.

"The Lord is my Shepherd." The Jehovah of the Old Testament is the Jesus of the New Testament.

When we say "Jehovah", we speak of **His Deity,** but when we say "Shepherd", we speak of **His Humanity.** In John 10, the Lord Jesus unlocked the mystery of the 23rd Psalm when He said: *"I am the good shepherd"*. *"I am"* - that is His Deity; *"the good shepherd"* - that is His Humanity. In the Lord Jesus, we have sovereignty and sympathy, a King and a Shepherd, a God who is able and a Shepherd who is available, a God in the heavens and a Shepherd in our hearts. *"The LORD, Jehovah, is my shepherd."*

Now do you ever think about: *(a) OUR SHEPHERD CARE?*

The word that is actually used for *"shepherd"* means: *"to tend the flock"*. It speaks of the role of the shepherd and his care for the flock. A shepherd would actually live with his sheep, twenty four hours a day, with unwavering devotion, day and night, both in fair weather and foul, to nurture, guide and protect his sheep. The shepherd would assume full responsibility for the needs and safety of his flock, even risking his own life for their protection.

Is this not what God has chosen to be towards His people? He watches over us. He walks with us. He works for us. He witnesses to us. His care for us is unchanging. It is unbroken. It is unlimited. It is unstinted. It is unending.

Then, there is: *(b) OUR SHEPHERD CHRIST*.

Three times in the New Testament the Lord Jesus is described as a shepherd.

Firstly, Christ is described as **THE GOOD SHEPHERD**. The Lord Jesus said: *"I am the good shepherd: the good shepherd giveth His life for the sheep"* (John 10 verse 11).

Now any shepherd may lose his life for the sheep, but Christ said: *"The good shepherd giveth* (or *layeth down*) *His life for the sheep"*. Did you know that there has only ever been one person who has chosen to die? Only One. You might say: *"What about suicides or martyrs, people dying for causes?"* I maintain that no-one has ever chosen to die, except the Lord Jesus. He was the only one who did not have to die. All the rest of us will die sooner or later. Some may just choose to die a little sooner than might otherwise be the case, but no-one has chosen to die - except one and that one was Christ. He laid down His life. Do you recall what He said? *"No man taketh it from Me"* (John 10 verse 18).

It was not nails that kept Him on the tree, but the silver cords of love. Now we have often heard of sheep dying for the shepherd who wants the sheep for food, but we are less likely to hear of any shepherd dying for the sheep.

But think of what Charles Wesley wrote:

Chapter 1

"That Thou my God should'st die for me."

When as the Good Shepherd He laid down His life for the sheep, He dealt with the *Penalty of Sin*. The *"wages of sin is death"* (Romans 6 verse 23) and that is what Christ paid. Your sin will be pardoned in Christ or punished in Hell, but it will never be overlooked. Unless you have a Good Shepherd who died for your sins, you will face the wrath of an angry God.

Secondly, Christ is described as **THE GREAT SHEPHERD**. In Hebrews 13 verse 20, we read: *"Now the God of peace, that brought again from the dead our Lord Jesus, that great shepherd of the sheep"*. That speaks of resurrection. In John 10, the Good Shepherd **died**, but in Hebrews 13, the Great Shepherd, **rose** for the sheep. What good is a dead shepherd? Christ carried our sin to the Cross and there He took care of the **penalty of our sin**, but when He rose from the dead He now deals with the **power of sin**. He is not only the Good Shepherd - He had to be good to die for our sins - but He is the Great Shepherd - He rose from the dead. That makes Him the Great Shepherd and the Bible says now He is able to lead us in *"paths of righteousness"* (Psalm 23 verse 3). He died for me. But now He lives for me.

Thirdly, however, Christ is described as **THE CHIEF SHEPHERD**. In 1 Peter 5 verse 4, we read: *"And when the chief Shepherd shall appear"*.

John 10 speaks of **Death**. Hebrews 13 speaks of **Resurrection**. 1 Peter 5 speaks of **Glory**. As the Good Shepherd, He had to be Good to do it, He died for us. As the Great Shepherd, He had to be Great to do it, He rose for us. But as the Chief Shepherd, He is coming to take us from the **presence of sin**.

Psalm 23 occupies a special position. It comes after Psalm 22 and before Psalm 24. You might say: "That is not very profound!" However, these three Psalms form a kind of trinity. In Psalm 22, we have the crucifixion of Christ. It is written as if a man was standing at the foot of the Cross. In Psalm 22, we have the Good Shepherd **dying** for the Sheep. In Psalm 23, the Great Shepherd is

From Earth to Glory

leading the Sheep. He is risen from the dead. Then, in Psalm 24, what do we find? The Chief Shepherd **coming** for the sheep.

So, in these 3 Psalms, you see the Good, the Great, and the Chief Shepherd. As the Good Shepherd, He died to pay the *Penalty of sin*. As the Great Shepherd, He rose to take care of the *Power of sin*. As the Chief Shepherd, He is coming to take us away from the *Presence of sin*.

Psalm 22 takes us to Mount Calvary. Psalm 24 centres around Mount Zion. Between them - where we are living now - is the valley of Psalm 23, where the Shepherd ministers to us.

Do you notice that almost all the verbs in this Psalm are in the present tense? This is a Psalm for you today. He makes me. He leads me. He restores. He guides. He is with me. He comforts me. He prepares a table for me. He anoints me. My cup overflows. His shepherding ministries are for me today.

How good to see in this first verse *The Majesty of the Sovereign* and *The Ministry of the Shepherd*. There is, however, a third feature in this first verse:

(3) THE MENTALITY OF THE SHEEP.

"I shall not want." What a bold statement to make!

Obviously, this is the sentiment of a sheep utterly satisfied with its owner, perfectly content with its lot in life.

We have often been blessed by the hymns of Fanny Crosby. Blind from six weeks old, she died at the age of 95. During her life, she composed 3,000 hymns, many of which remain favourites to this day.

One of the greatest verses that ever came from her pen was something that she wrote at 8 years of age. Ponder carefully her words:

Chapter 1

> *"Oh, what a happy soul am I,*
> *Although I cannot see,*
> *I am resolved that in this world*
> *Contented I will be.*
> *How many blessings I enjoy*
> *That other people don't!*
> *To weep and sigh because I'm blind,*
> *I cannot, and I won't."*

Happy, contented and satisfied. Do you know many of the Lord's flock that are like that?

There is here: **(a) A PERSONAL SATISFACTION.**

One little boy was quoting this Psalm. He got mixed up and so he said: *"The Lord is my Shepherd and I've got all I want"*. David looks back on his journey through life and he says that his Shepherd had met his every need.

When David Ben-Gurion, the first Prime Minister of Israel, was facing a series of crises in his young nation, someone asked what he needed. He said: *"The only things we need are things which begin with the letter 'A'"*. Then he went on to explain: *"A lot of tanks. A lot of money. A lot of guns. A lot of food."*

'I shall not want' does not mean that if the Lord is our Shepherd, we will have everything we want. It means we will not want for anything we need. So many believers misunderstand Psalm 37 verse 4: *"Delight thyself also in the LORD; and He shall give thee the desires of thine heart"*. They think that it means that if you love the Saviour, you can have a Rolls Royce. No! No! Rather, when you delight yourself in the Lord, the deepest desires of your heart will be met.

There is here: **(b) A SPIRITUAL REALISATION.**

Do you know what that realisation is? It is not so much *what* God gives, but what God *is* that will satisfy. He Himself is my satisfaction. Now when a man can say: *"Jehovah is my Shepherd"* and mean it, he has discovered the secret of satisfaction and contentment. Now do you see what David does here? He takes the name "Shepherd" and links it with the name "Jehovah". *"Jehovah my Shepherd."* The Hebrew says: **"Jehovah-raah."** That is one of the names of God.

Seven times in the Old Testament, we find certain words attached to Jehovah which together with the name "Jehovah" convey a wonderful revelation of God?

1. In Psalm 23 verse 1 - Jehovah-raah - "The Lord my Shepherd".
2. In Genesis 22 verse 13 - Jehovah-jireh - "The Lord will provide".
3. In Exodus 15 verse 26 - Jehovah-rapha - "The Lord that healeth".
4. In Judges 6 verse 24 - Jehovah-shalom - "The Lord our Peace".
5. In Jeremiah 23 verse 6 - Jehovah-tsidkenu - "The Lord our Righteousness".
6. In Ezekiel 48 verse 35 - Jehovah-shammah - "The Lord ever Present".
7. In Exodus 17 verse 15 - Jehovah-nissi - "The Lord our Banner".

Now look at Psalm 23 again:

"The Lord .... my Shepherd." Who is that? That is Jehovah-raah.

"I shall not want." Who is that? That is Jehovah-jireh. The Lord will provide.

" He maketh to lie .... waters." Who is that? That is Jehovah-shalom. The Lord our Peace.

"He restoreth my soul." Who is that? That is Jehovah-rapha. The Lord who heals.

"He leadeth me in the paths of righteousness." Who is that? That is Jehovah-tsidkenu. The Lord our Righteousness.

"Thou preparest a table before me in the presence of mine enemies." Who is that? That is Jehovah-nissi. The Lord our Banner.

"Yea, thou I walk through the valley of the shadow of death, I will fear no

Chapter 1

evil for Thou art with me." Who is that? That is Jehovah-shammah. The Lord ever Present.

You see all of these seven wonderful names, all of these seven wonderful provisions are gathered up in this 23rd Psalm. Happy is the person who knows this all-sufficient Shepherd, Saviour and Friend.

In Him and in Him alone is the secret of satisfaction and contentment.

Not the things He gives me! The things He gives me are only a representation of who the Lord is Himself. ***No, it is He Himself, who is the secret of satisfaction.*** Jehovah is my Shepherd - I have got all I want.

Is the Lord your Shepherd? Is He? Do you want to know how you can find out? *Is the Shepherd your Lord?* The only way for you to be able to say: "The Lord is my Shepherd" is for you to be able to say: "The Shepherd is my Lord".

Years ago, a preacher came upon a shepherd-boy tending his sheep. Sitting down beside him, the preacher asked the young Scottish boy if he knew the 23rd Psalm. *"Of course I do"*, the boy replied. *"Then what is the opening sentence"*, asked the preacher. The boy replied: *"The Lord is my Shepherd"*.

The preacher asked the shepherd-boy to tick off a finger for each word. Beginning with his thumb and ending with his little finger. Then he explained to this boy how he could make Christ his Saviour. Before he left, the boy received Christ as his Saviour, and the preacher left him clutching hard at his fourth finger - *"my."* The following winter was severe and one day the boy and his sheep did not come home. They were all caught and buried in a deep snow drift. When those who came searching started to dig, they discovered the bodies of many dead sheep, and the body of the wee lad, lying on his back, peace on his face, the fourth finger in his left hand, grasped by his right hand. Such was his last thought!

Can you truthfully say this: ***"The LORD is my Shepherd"***?
You may know the Psalm, but do you know the Shepherd?

CHAPTER 2

Success Over Stress

Robert Orben once said: *"Sometimes I get the feeling the whole world is against me, but deep down I know that it is not true. Some of the smaller countries are neutral"*.

Do you ever feel that the whole world is against you? Do you ever feel pressed in body and pressed in soul? One stressed-out secretary told her boss: *"When this rush is over, I am going to have a nervous breakdown. I earned it. I deserve it and nobody is going to take it from me"*.

The sheep in the Middle East get up and begin to browse and graze about 4 o'clock in the morning. The shepherd begins to lead them out of the sheepfold while the dew is still on the grass and all around is very quiet. The sheep will graze and nibble there and then about 10 o'clock or 11 o'clock in the morning, when the sun is very hot, the shepherd will find some secluded spot with green pastures and allow the sheep to lie down. They will lie there for 3 or 4 hours and just chew the cud.

It is at that time when the sheep are lying down and are quiet, when they are digesting what they have ingested, when they are chewing the cud, it is at that time that the sheep are growing the fattest. It is then that they are putting on fat and wool, and are maturing.

Every shepherd knows how important it is for his sheep to have a quiet time. Do you see how David puts it? *"He maketh me to lie down in green pastures: He leadeth me beside the still waters."*

Chapter 2

This verse helps us understand **Success Over Stress.** Is stress ever a problem to you? So many people are all stressed up, tense, running about, so busy, so much in a hurry. Sometimes, we think it is wrong for us to be quiet and still.

A lady phoned her pastor up and said: *"Pastor, I tried to ring you all day on Monday and I could not get you"*. *"Well,"* he said, *"Monday is my day off. I was resting"*. She said: *"The devil never takes time off."* He said: *"Yes, and if I didn't, I would be just like the devil!"*

God wants His sheep to learn how to get quiet, to lie down in the green pastures and to drink at the still waters. Now, there are plenty of rushing waters in the Middle East but the sheep are afraid to drink there. However, they will drink when the water gets into a quiet pool. So: *"He leadeth me beside the still waters."*

Do you know the reason why we are so tense, why we are so pressed out of measure? Because we are like sheep! The Psalmist says: *"We are the sheep of His pasture"* (Psalm 100 verse 3). You say: *"Is that not wonderful? I am a sheep"*. Well, God was not trying to compliment us when He said that. This is not really a compliment. It is a description. *"We are the sheep of His pasture."*

When you think about a sheep, you realise that a sheep is not one of the smartest animals around. In fact, it is overloaded with **Dumbness**. It really is! How many of you have seen a circus with a trained sheep? Horses are trained. Lions, monkeys, elephants, but not a sheep. Why? Because a sheep is not too smart. You might say: *"I was top of my class!"* You misunderstand. I am talking in spiritual terms. When Christ spoke to Nicodemus, that man was intellectually at the top of his class but spiritually he was ignorant. As Paul puts it in Romans 3 verse 11: "There is none that understandeth". We are like sheep. We are dumb.

But then a sheep is also **Defenceless.** They are helpless, timid creatures, whose only recourse is to run. Other animals can defend themselves. A mule will kick; a lion will bite; a skunk - well you know what a skunk can do! A sheep is pretty defenceless. Isaiah 53 verse 7 pictures the Lord Jesus as a lamb being brought to the slaughter, *"and as a sheep before her shearers is dumb"*. You think of sheep as needing someone to protect them. And that is the way we are. That is why Paul says in 2 Corinthians 3 verse 5: *"Our sufficiency is of God"*. We do not have it in and of ourselves.

Moreover, a sheep does not have a good sense of **Direction.** It is easily lost. Isaiah says: *"All we like sheep have gone astray"* (Isaiah 53 verse 6). Sheep nibble and browse here and there. They can then get further from the flock and the shepherd. Then they are lost. That is bad enough, but what is worse – the sheep cannot find their way home. Sheep need to be sought and brought.

Do you recall what God said about His people in Hosea 11 verse 7: *"My people are bent to backsliding from Me"*. We have a tendency to get away from God.

In his hymn: "Come, Thou Fount of every blessing", Robert Robinson wrote:

> *"Prone to wander, Lord, I feel it,*
> *Prone to leave the God I love."*

That is the sheep nature, but while a sheep is **Dumb, Defenceless, Directionless,** it is also **Dependent** on the shepherd.

Phillip Keller, a shepherd himself, tells us that a sheep can become "cast". This happens when it rolls over on its back and cannot get up. After a few hours, its circulation is cut off and the sheep will die. A cast sheep is also vulnerable to vultures and wolves. Did David have that in mind when he said: *"Why art thou cast down, O my soul?"* (Psalm 42 verse 11)?

We get into a <u>**cast**</u> position and the Shepherd needs to come and pick us up and put us on our feet again. Has He ever done that for you? When you were <u>**down**</u> and you could not get up? How thankful we should be to God for the shepherd! Yes, we are like sheep, and because of this we have a tendency to be stressed. Now, how do you handle stress? How can you be successful over stress?

Chapter 2

Psalm 23 verse 2 provides the answer. We can be stress-free when we allow:

(1) THE SHEPHERD'S PRESENCE TO CONSOLE US.

Sheep will refuse to lie down unless they are free of all fear. The growl of a lion, the bark of a dog, the presence of a little child will be sufficient to spoil the rest of a flock of sheep and cause a stampede. As long as there is the slightest suspicion of danger from dogs, cougars, and bears, the sheep will stand up and get ready to flee for their lives. It is only the presence of the shepherd that quietens and reassures them and puts them at ease.

Notice what David says: *"He maketh me .... He leadeth me"*. Who is the *He*? *"Jehovah my Shepherd."* It has already been said that the Jehovah of the Old Testament is the Jesus of the New Testament. Christ is the Good, Great, and Chief Shepherd and there is nothing like the presence of the Shepherd to dispel the fear, the terror, of the unknown.

How do you handle stress? David says: *"He maketh me .... He leadeth me ...."*. You see, it's impossible for sheep to *"lie down,"* unless certain requirements are met.

The first such requirement is: *(a) The Fears of the Sheep Must be Dealt With.*

Sheep are very nervous animals. They are easily frightened. Even a rabbit suddenly bounding from behind a bush can stampede a whole flock. Now their fears are not relieved by the absence of danger, their fears are relieved by *the Presence of the Shepherd.* There is nothing that so reassures the sheep as to see the presence of the shepherd in the field. We live in a most uncertain age and we cannot possibly remove every danger or threat. Any hour can bring disaster, danger and distress from unknown quarters. Life is full of hazards. No-one can tell what a day may bring forth. But, bless God, the fears of the sheep can be dealt with by the Shepherd. Our Lord Jesus Christ came from Heaven to earth to defeat death, hell and the grave and to conquer every fear. He is the Victor over all. In His earthly ministry, He proved His power over _disease_ - He healed the sick. He proved His power over _demons_ - He cast them out. He proved His power over _death_ - He raised the dead. He proved His power over the _Devil_ - He defeated him.

On Calvary He completed His victory over death, hell and the grave as He rose from the dead on the third day. He is alive forevermore! He declares: *"I am He that liveth, and was dead; and, behold, I am alive for evermore, Amen; and have the keys of hell and of death"* (Revelation 1 verse 18). Do you need rest from fears? What is your fear? Do you fear a person or some circumstance? Do you fear your inability? Do you fear the unknown future? Will you allow your fears to dispel in the presence of your Shepherd?

Then: **(b) The Friction of the Sheep Must be Dealt With.**

Sheep are contrary animals, much like people. They establish an order among themselves. Chickens have a *"pecking order."* Cattle have a *"horning order"* and sheep have a *"butting order."* Usually there will be some arrogant, cunning and domineering old ewe who will be the boss of any bunch of sheep. She will seek to maintain her position of prestige by butting and driving away other ewes or lambs from the best grazing or favourite bedding grounds. This causes uneasiness amongst the whole flock. The sheep become edgy, tense, discontented and restless. But whenever the shepherd appears, rivalries are forgotten and quarrels are ended.

Is there not friction among God's sheep? We always seem to be butting one another. *"I don't like what she said!" "I don't like what they have!" "I don't like how they treated my child!"* We are always butting. There is always friction. But then the Shepherd steps on the scene. When we consciously abide in the presence of the Shepherd, the friction ceases. I wonder - are you angry with some believer? Irritated because of them? Is it because you have taken your eyes off the Shepherd? Is it because you have left Christ out of the picture?

Then: **(c) The Flies of the Sheep Must be Dealt With.**

Chapter 2

The sheep will never lie down if they are tormented by flies or parasites. Only when free of these pests can they relax. A good shepherd will apply various types of insect-repellents to his sheep. He will see that they are dipped to clear their fleeces of ticks. The shepherd will see that there is enough shelter in the trees and bush where the sheep can find refuge and release from their tormentors.

In the Christian life, there are many irritations. But is there an antidote for them? Can we get to the place of quiet contentment despite them? Yes! Is this not one of the functions of the Holy Spirit? The Holy Spirit is often symbolized in Scripture by oil. Oil is that which brings healing and comfort from the harsh and abrasive aspects of life. Is there something disturbing you? Do you need to go to the Lord and say: *"Lord, this is beyond me. I can't cope with it. I can't rest - please take over"*.

But there is something else that needs to happen before a sheep will *"lie down"*.

(d) The Famine of the Sheep Must be Dealt With.

A sheep that is hungry will never lie down. A hungry, ill-fed sheep is ever on its feet, always on the move, seeking to satisfy its gnawing hunger. Now *"green pastures"* did not just happen by chance. Green pastures were the product of hard labour, time and skill in land-use. But it was the shepherd's responsibility to provide food for his sheep.

Do you see here the wonderful ministry of our Shepherd? Our fears are dealt with by our Shepherd. Our friction is dealt with by the Shepherd. The flies, the irritations of life, dealt with by the Shepherd. The inner longings of our soul met by the ministry of the Shepherd. Do we want success over stress? Well, allow the Shepherd's presence to console us.

(2) THE SHEPHERD'S PROVISION TO CONTENT US.

Does the Psalmist say: *"He maketh me to lie down in brown, withered pastures"?* Is that it? Or: *"He leadeth me beside muddy streams"?* Oh, no! That is not how our Shepherd provides. It is *"green pastures and still waters"*. All I need - and more - I find in the Lord Jesus. Now, why do we get stressed? Because we think our needs are not going to be met. Yet our Shepherd provides for us:

(a) MATERIALLY.

When David says: *"He maketh ... to lie down in green pastures"*, he means that the sheep have already grazed to their fill. They are full; they are satisfied; their needs have all been met, and they are resting in the blessing. If the Lord is our Shepherd, He will see to it that in one way or another all our needs are met. Are you stressed out because of material needs? Do you recall that in Matthew's Gospel our Lord Jesus tells us on three occasions: *"Take no thought"* (Matthew 6 verses 25, 31 and 34)? In other words: *"Stop worrying!"* What do people worry about today? *Food, finance, family, fashion and fitness.* That is what people worry about, and do you know what the Lord Jesus said? *"After all these things do the Gentiles (the unsaved) seek"* (Matthew 6 verse 32).

Christ is not saying these things are not important, but what He is saying is this: *"Seek ye first the kingdom of God, and His righteousness; and all these things shall be added unto you"* (Matthew 6 verse 33). You might say: *"If I get involved in the kingdom and chasing holiness, then what happens?"* *"All these things .... you."* Get your priorities right and all the rest will fall into place.

Indeed these things do not even take on significance until your deepest needs are met. You see, our Shepherd not only provides for us *materially* but also:

(b) SPIRITUALLY.

When David said: *"He maketh me to lie down in green pastures: He leadeth me beside the still waters"*, what did he mean? Is he talking about having your bank account full? No!

Think again of Psalms 22, 23, and 24 as a trinity of Psalms. Go back to Psalm 22 verse 26: "The meek shall eat and shall be satisfied". Look at Psalm 22 verse 29: "All they that be fat upon earth shall eat and worship". God wants healthy sheep.

What do the *"green pastures"* speak of? The *"green pastures"* of His Word. What do *"the still waters"* speak of? The still waters of His Spirit. You see, we find satisfaction in the Lord. If you do not find contentment there, you will be stressed - and I will tell you why. The deepest needs of your heart will not be met. Do you recall the words of the Lord Jesus? *"Man shall not live by bread alone, but by every word that proceedeth out of the mouth of God"* (Matthew 4 verse 4). The Bible is to you what bread is to the natural man. Here is the cure for stress. *"The green pastures"* of His Word. *"Green pastures"* are a biblical image of God's Word. It is interesting that the word *"pastor"* is related to the word *"pasture."* What is a pastor? He is someone who leads the flock into the green pastures of Scripture. Do you recall Peter's word to the elders? *"Feed the flock of God which is among you"* (1 Peter 5 verse 2). In the book of Jeremiah, God says: *"And I will give you pastors according to Mine heart, which shall feed you with knowledge and understanding"* (Jeremiah 3 verse 15). C.H. Spurgeon says: *"What are these 'green pastures' but the Scriptures of truth, always fresh, always rich, and never exhausted? Sweet and full are the doctrines of the gospel; fit food for souls, as tender grass is natural nutriment for sheep".*

When Israel were passing through the Wilderness, they fed on the manna and concerning it we read: *"They gathered it every morning"* (Exodus 16 verse 21). Do you rise each morning to gather the heavenly manna? I am greatly impressed with that word that God spoke to Moses in Exodus 34 verse 2: *"Be ready in the morning".*

The biographies of great men and women of God repeatedly point out that the secret of success in their spiritual life can be attributed to the *"morning hours."* Thomas Chalmers, the founding father of the Free Church of Scotland, entered the pulpit as an ordained modernist. Whenever the elders came to see him he was always at his books, books of astronomy, science, and so on. One day Thomas Chalmers got gloriously saved - and when the elders then came to see him, they said: "Thomas, we see now you have only one book and you never let it from your desk. It is the 'Book of God'".

If you were to take a spiritual medical today, how is your appetite for the Word of God? Are you ready in the morning to meet with God in the light of His Word and in the atmosphere of prayer? What do we know about *"the green pastures"* of His Word and the *"still waters"* of His Spirit?

Do you recall the cry of our Good Shepherd? *"If any man thirst, let him come unto Me, and drink. He that believeth on Me, as the Scriptures hath said, out of his belly shall flow rivers of living water."* John then gives the explanation: *"But this spake He of the Spirit, which they that believe on Him should receive"* (John 7 verses 37 to 39).

The Bible teaches that we are born again through the power of the Holy Spirit (John 3 verses 5 to 8) and that He indwells every believer (Romans 8 verse 9). The Spirit empowers us to live holy lives as we depend on Him (Galatians 5 verses 16 to 23). He gives us hope in the trials of life (Romans 5 verses 3 to 5 and Romans 15 verse 13). He guides us (Acts 13 verses 2 to 4 and Acts 16 verses 6 and 7). He teaches us (1 John 2 verse 27). He prays for us (Romans 8 verse 26). He gives us help and comfort (John 14 verse 16 and John 15 verse 26). He gives us spiritual gifts (1 Corinthians 12 verses 7 to 11) and empowers us to bear witness of Jesus Christ throughout the world (Acts 1 verse 8). With such a full provision of living water from our Good Shepherd, why do we try to quench our thirst with the polluted, broken cisterns of the world?

Phillip Keller tells us sometimes stubborn sheep will not wait for the clear, pure water that the shepherd is leading them to. They stop to drink from the polluted potholes along the trail, contaminated with the manure and urine of previous flocks. It satisfies their thirst for the moment, but it will eventually riddle them with parasites and disease. It is the price they pay for instant gratification, rather than following the shepherd to clear water.

Are you like those stubborn sheep? You want a quick fix. Instant happiness - so you go for the polluted potholes of the world.

Chapter 2

You say: *"What harm can it do?"* or: *"Who can it hurt?"* Do you not realize that the consequences of sin are often delayed? Seeds sown to the flesh can take a while to sprout. Do not be deceived. Whatever you sow, you reap. If you want: *"Success over Stress"*, learn to walk in the Spirit, God's gracious provision for you.

"He maketh ... to lie down in green pastures" – that is **His Word.** *"He leadeth me beside the still waters"* – that is **His Spirit.**

How can I handle stress? I need the Shepherd's presence to console me and the Shepherd's provision to content me.

There is a third benefit:

(3) THE SHEPHERD'S PEACE TO CONTROL US.

No sight so satisfies the shepherd as to see his flock well, quietly-fed, able to lie down to rest and to ruminate. Of course, sheep will not lie down until they are content. They will not lie down in *"green pastures"* or anywhere else if they are troubled, insecure or frightened. Sheep only lie down when they feel secure, content and at peace. *"He maketh me to lie down."* That is a picture of peace, contentment and serenity.

Do you ever think of: *(a) THE LACK OF CONTENTMENT IN THE WORLD?*

The word *"contentment"* comes from two Latin words: *"con"* and *"tenio"*. It means: *"to hold together"* which is the opposite of falling to pieces. Contentment is saying: *"The world may coming apart at the seams, but I am holding together because of Christ"*.

Coming downstairs one morning, a British nobleman heard his cook exclaim: *"Oh, if I only had five pounds, wouldn't I be content?"* Wishing to satisfy the woman, soon afterwards he handed her a five pound note. She thanked him profusely. But, after he stepped out of the room again, he overheard her say: *"Why didn't I say ten?"*

37

How much do we need to be happy? Just a little bit more than we have got. A reporter asked the late oil tycoon, J. Paul Getty: *"If you retired now, would you say that your holdings would be worth a billion dollars?"* Getty did some mental calculations. *"I suppose so"*, he said, *"but remember, a billion doesn't go as far these days as it used to"*. Never content! Constantly striving after more things, living on credit, and widespread restlessness. Even many of God's people are not content, yet the Bible says that God has provided us with everything pertaining to life and godliness (2 Peter 1 verse 3). We are to be content with His provision.

Yet people are ever on the move. You can stand in an airport and watch a fly past. I do not mean the planes! I mean the people going in all directions. The story is told about an U.S.A. fighter plane that fired its canon and was moving so fast that it literally overtook the bullet and shot itself down. The plane was moving faster than the shell.

There are a lot of folks who are doing the same thing. They are shooting themselves down. They are not taking time to *"lie down"*.

There is a Lack of Contentment in the World, but think about: *(b)* ***THE LIFE OF CONTENTMENT IN THE LORD.***

Psalm 23 is the Psalm of a contented heart. *"He maketh me to lie down."* Do you know what the sheep is doing when it is lying down? It is chewing the cud. A sheep has a second stomach and it puts that sweet, green grass down there in that second stomach. It is loading up and then the shepherd says: *"Lie down - digest what you have got"*. So the sheep brings it back up to taste it. That is when the sheep is growing. That is the most productive time for the sheep - that serenity, that quiet time.

Now if the *"green pastures"* are the Word of God, what is the sheep doing when it is chewing the cud? It is meditating. *"In His law doth he meditate day and night."* (Psalm 1 verse 2. See also Psalm 19 verse 14; Psalm 104 verse 34 and Psalm 119 verse 35). Do you know what is wrong with most of us? We do not lie down in the green pastures and meditate.

Chapter 2

Most of us think we have done the Lord a favour by coming to church! Some cannot even do that! But when you go home, do you really meditate? Do you chew the cud? Why, you say: *"I am too busy."* If you are too busy for this, then you are busier than God intended you to be. Now I am not against business, but do you need to stop and prioritise your life? Do you know what God does with some of us? He **makes** us to lie down. We do not do it, unless He makes us. David said: *"Before I was afflicted I went astray: but now have I kept Thy Word"* (Psalm 119 verse 67).

"He maketh me." But why do you not do it yourself? Why do you not say: *"I want to be still. I want to know that He is God"?* How do you deal with stress? Remember a distressed sheep is not producing. It is not producing wool or fat. It is not reproducing. *"He maketh me to lie down."* Why does the Shepherd do that? Because He wants healthy sheep. Do you want ***"Success over Stress"***? Then we must allow:

1. The Shepherd's Presence To Console Us;
2. The Shepherd's Provision To Content Us;
3. The Shepherd's Peace To Control Us.

A little boy yelled: *"Mummy"*.
His mother shouted back from the kitchen: *"What is it, Johnny?"*
The little boy answered: *"You know that special dish you always worried about?"*
"Yes, Dear, what about it?"
The little boy shouted: *"You don't have to worry about it anymore!"*

With the Shepherd's Presence with you; the Shepherd's Provision before you, and the Shepherds' Peace within you - all will be well.

You don't have to worry about it anymore!

CHAPTER 3

The Ministry Of Restoration

A humorous story is told about two students who got a summer job with a Highway Department. They were given the job of painting the centre lines of a rural road. The supervisor told them that they were on probation, and that they must stay above the average of two miles per day to keep their job. One the first day they completed four miles. *Yet, on their second day they only completed two miles.* Their supervisor was somewhat concerned with the drop in their progress but didn't say anything because they were still at average. However, on the third day, the students only did one mile. The supervisor decided that he needed to talk to them so he called them in and said: *"Boys, you did so well on your first day and although the second day was not as good, you did the average. But today you only did one mile. You are doing less each day. What seems to be the problem?"* The students replied: ***"We are getting further and further from the bucket!"***

A humorous story, but it teaches a valuable lesson. Do you find yourself getting further and further away - from the Lord? The Psalmist said in Psalm 119 verse 176: *"I have gone astray like a lost sheep".*

Could it be that you are wandering from the God of the Word and the Word of God? Are you like a cast sheep? Sometimes a sheep - often a heavy or overweight one - will decide to lie down in a little hollow or depression in the field. If it moves too far it gets into a position where its feet no longer touch the ground. Lying on its back, its feet in the air, the sheep flays away frantically, struggling to stand up without success. There is an old shepherding maxim that says: *"A down sheep is a dead sheep"*. A cast sheep can perish in a matter of hours unless the shepherd finds it and restores it. Are you cast down? Is your world upside down? Are you unable to right yourself? Do you need to experience the ministry of restoration?

Even the very best of God's servants are prone to wander. It is the nature of the sheep to get out of fellowship with the shepherd. Many of us become what the Bible calls *"backsliders"*. Now, backsliders are not lost. A backslider is a saved person who is out of fellowship with God, but he is not lost. Indeed God says that He is married to the backslider (Jeremiah 3 verses 11 to 15).

There is a bond there that cannot be broken but while that <u>Relationship</u> cannot be broken, the <u>Fellowship</u> can. The joy can be lost. David himself had become a *cast* sheep. He had tasted defeat in his life and that is why he prayed in Psalm 51: *"Restore unto me the joy of Thy salvation"*. David did not lose his salvation, but he lost the joy of it. He lost the joy of it and he wanted to be restored. God did restore him and David could say: *"He restoreth my soul"* (verse 3).

It is beneficial to see how the Lord restores us. Here are three wonderful truths that will get us right with God and will keep us right with God.

(1) THE PROCESS OF RESTORATION

"He restoreth my soul."

The word *"restore"* means: *"to bring again"* or *"to bring home"*. The Hebrew word here means: *"to bring back"*.

There are three kinds of sheep that need to be restored. There is the **Stubborn Sheep.** Do you know any stubborn sheep? There are stubborn sheep who just want their own way. We think of a sheep as being gentle and docile, but sometimes a sheep can be very stubborn. They want to go their own way. Isaiah 53 verse 6 declares: *"All we like sheep have gone astray; we have turned every one to his own way"*. Turning "to my own way" means "doing what I want".

It implies that I feel free to assert my own wishes and carry out my own ideas. This I do in spite of every warning! Stubborn - and we need to be restored.

Then there is the **Straying Sheep**. They do not wilfully go away - they just weakly go away. They carelessly get away and fall into pits and crevices, or get entangled in thorns. They need to be brought back.

Then again there is the **Sick Sheep.** There are many dangers out there! Diseases and poison. Sheep can get very sick - and they need to be restored.

It is the Shepherd who restores these sheep. See how he does it. Well, he has three instruments. They are all spoken of in the Psalm. He has got a rod, a staff and oil. He uses these three things to restore the sheep.

He restores *THE STUBBORN SHEEP WITH THE ROD.*

This is the Ministry of Chastisement. What was the shepherd's rod? Well, the shepherd would go out and he would find a young sapling, a little tree. He would dig it up by the roots, and the roots would be all sticking out from a knob. He would work at it until it was smooth and then he would take that knob that was right at the end and he would hammer nails and bits of metal into it until it was weighted. It became a very powerful club, a weapon in his hand.

The shepherd would be out there on the hillsides for many weeks and, of course, he would practise throwing that rod. He would throw it and throw it until it became a deadly missile. He also learned to wield it and use it as a club. It was used to protect himself from the robbers. It was used to protect the sheep from lions and wolves, but sometimes he had to use the rod on the

Chapter 3

sheep himself and the rod would be a form of chastisement to the sheep.

If there would be a very stubborn sheep, the shepherd would do something very **drastic.** He would take the rod and break one of the legs of that sheep and after he had done that he would immediately bind it and put it in a splint. He would wrap it up and try to heal the sheep. He would carry that sheep on his shoulders until that leg was mended. Oh, he would nurture that sheep and pour in the oil and when the leg was healed, he would restore the sheep to its feet again. Then an interesting thing would happen. That sheep that had been broken and healed would stay very close to the shepherd, by his side. Indeed, that sheep would be the file-leader who would lead the other sheep.

A lady visited Switzerland and observed a sheepfold located high on a mountainside. She noticed an individual sheep by the side of the road, bleating in pain. Looking more closely, she discovered that its leg was injured. She asked the shepherd how it happened. *"I had to break it myself"*, he answered sadly. *"It was the only way I could keep that wayward creature from straying into unsafe places. From past experience I have found that a sheep will follow me once I have nursed it back to health. Because of the loving relationship that will be established as I care for her, in the future she will come instantly at my beck and call."*

The one who had been broken and then the one who had been restored. Do you recall what God says in the book of Hosea? *"Come, and let us return to the Lord: for He hath torn, and He will heal us; He hath smitten, and He will bind us up"* (Hosea 6 verse 1). The same God who **breaks us** is the God who **binds us** in order that we might return to Him. Is this not what David meant when he said: *"Before I was afflicted, I went astray: but now have I kept Thy Word .... it is good for me that I have been afflicted"* (Psalm 119 verses 67 and 71). Broken that he might be blessed. Now does God apply the rod of chastisement because He does not love the sheep? No! He applies it because He does love them (see Hebrews 12 verses 5 to 11). It was not a joyful thing when a sheep got its leg broken, yet it brought peace and fruitfulness to the shepherd. What was the fruit? *"He restoreth my soul"* (Psalm 23 verse 3).

Sometimes, when you are a stubborn sheep, God applies the rod of chastisement.

You are not to despise it for this kind of chastening does 3 things as Dr. Adrian Rogers, famous pastor of Bellevue Baptist Church, Memphis, pointed out.

1. It Reveals Your Sonship (Hebrews 12 verse 6)
The shepherd loved the sheep. That is why he applied the rod. *"Scourging,"* is not a 'spanking' but something very severe. Sometimes it takes that - does it not? You say: *"Well, I dabble in sin: go my own way: and run with the world and God does not chastise me"*. In Hebrews 12 verse 8, God says: *"You are not My child, if you were My child I would have chastened you .... you are illegitimate, you are claiming to be Mine when you are not, 'for whom the Lord loveth, He chasteneth'"*.

2. It Renews Your Worship (Hebrews 12 verses 9 to 10)
God is not primarily in the business of making you happy or healthy but of making you holy. God saved you to make you holy, like Him.

3. It Restores Your Fellowship (Hebrews 12 verses 11)
Of course, at the time it is not joyful. When you were a child and your father had to punish you, did you say: *"Why, this is wonderful!"*? Did you say that? No! *"No chastening .... afterward ...."* *"Before I was afflicted I went astray but now ...."* (Psalm 119 verse 67) Oh, that sheep that had its leg broken never wanted to stray from the shepherd again.

How does the Shepherd deal with the stubborn sheep? With the rod of chastisement. But, how does the Shepherd deal with the straying sheep?

He restores **THE STRAYING SHEEP WITH THE STAFF.**

This is the Ministry of Correction
The shepherd had not only

Chapter 3

a rod but a staff (verse 4). He would get another sapling and he would cut this one above the root. It would be long and willowy and he would take that staff while it was green, soak it in water, perhaps boiling water, till he could bend it and he would put a bend in the end of it and tie it. Then he would let it dry and season, and at the end he had it shaped just right. There was a crook, a bend, a curve just big enough to go around the chest of a little lamb or the neck of a sheep. Oh, he knew how to use it. He would be walking along and he would just touch the sheep with it. Put it around the neck of a sheep. Pull the sheep in that was straying. When they were walking along a narrow path and the sheep might fall over, he would use the staff just to guide the sheep. And when the sheep would get down in the briars and mud he would put the staff there and lift that sheep out.

Yes, he would use the staff to *guard, guide, lift, and retrieve the sheep to him.* Sometimes a ewe would neglect her lambs and the shepherd would take the crook and draw the lambs and the mother sheep back together again. How the Good Shepherd needs today to draw those mothers and fathers and children back together again when the devil is doing all he can to break up Christian homes. The Shepherd is guiding with His staff and when we get away from God and get into sin and get stuck in the briars and mud, He has that staff of love and grace. He draws us back to Him.

But what about the sick sheep?

He restores *THE SICK SHEEP WITH THE OIL.*

This is the Ministry of Comfort Each night, the shepherd would bring the sheep into the sheepfold and as they would come in each night here is what the shepherd would do. He would count them and call them by name and then he would caress them. He would put his hands all over the sheep and rub his fingers down into the wool and he would be looking for a scar, bruise, scab, laceration. If he found a cut, he not only had a rod and staff but a bottle of oil. He would anoint the head of that sheep with oil. The oil was there to soothe, heal, medicate, lubricate and give comfort to that wounded sheep.

The oil would be mixed with sulphur and tar. It was used to repel insects. Sheep have a pest that bothers them - *"nose flies"*. They get into wounds. This oil would be smeared on the nose to give comfort and protection from these pests. The oil of the Holy Spirit protects us from the devil's flies. There is comfort when we have been bruised, hurt and wounded. Our Shepherd calls His own sheep by name. He knows us. He cares for us. He feels with us. He comforts us when we have been hurt and wounded. He binds us up and brings us back to Himself.

I think that David had all these things in mind when he said: *"He restoreth my soul"*. David had been stubborn and broken. David had strayed and had been retrieved. David had been hurt and wounded. David had been healed by the Lord.

Bless God for the Good Shepherd's ministry of Chastisement – the rod; His ministry of Correction – the staff, and His ministry of Comfort – the oil.

(2) THE PURPOSE OF RESTORATION

"He restoreth my soul."

Why? In order that He might *"lead me in the paths of righteousness."*

Pastor Mullan preached at my induction service in Carryduff and he spoke on 1 Peter 5 verse 2: *"Feed the flock of God which is among you"*. He used three words as his three points. **Feed, Lead and Plead.** The shepherd is not only to feed the flock but to lead the flock. He restores us that He might master, lead and guide us. The problem with so many of us is all we are interested in is getting restored. *But if you do not go on from restoration to righteousness, you are going to be back in the same old problem.*

Many of us only want to get back right, but we do not want to get on the track of following God. That is the reason why we go back to where we were. But, a restored sheep ought to follow closer than ever before. We ought to be like the sheep with the broken leg that stays close to the shepherd, that He might master us and lead us so that we may never go astray again. When are we ever going to learn? How many times are we going to fall and slip before we stay close to the Shepherd? Here is the purpose of restoration: *"He restoreth my soul"*. Why? In order that He might *"lead me in the paths of righteousness"*.

(a) THE SHEPHERD HAS A PLAN FOR US

"He leadeth me." He has a plan. The shepherd is conscious at all times of the needs of the sheep. Where they need to go. What they need to eat. What they need to drink. His life is given to the sheep. Can you imagine how foolish an idea it would be for the sheep to attempt to lead the shepherd? Or for a sheep to lead other sheep? Or for a sheep to seek to lead itself? They must have a shepherd to lead them. How reassuring it is to know this: *"He leadeth me.*

How does He lead? Through the Word of God, through the Works of Providence, through the Witness of the Spirit, through the Wisdom of fellow believers.

"He leadeth me." In an uncertain age, when none of us knows what will happen in the next sixty seconds, we are put at ease knowing that our Good Shepherd is the same yesterday, today and forever. He knows the future as fully as He knows the past. He knows the plans He has for us and every twist and turn has been anticipated. *"He leadeth me."* The question is - are we following? Recall the words of the Lord Jesus: *"My sheep hear My voice and I know them and they follow Me"* (John 10 verse 27). Most of us, however, simply do not want to do this. We do not want to deny ourselves, to give up our right to make our own decisions. We do not want to follow. We do not want to be led. Is that you? Sure, we sing: *"He leadeth me"* or: *"Following Jesus ever day by day"*. We talk about being *"led of the Lord"* and give mental assent to the idea, but really how many of us are following His leading? Yet the Shepherd has a plan for us.

Notice again: **(b) THE SHEPHERD HAS A PATH FOR US.**

Where does He lead us? *"In the paths of righteousness."* (verse 3)

This phrase has a dual meaning. *"Paths of righteousness"* means:

1. Right Paths

If sheep are to be moved from field to field without falling into deep crevices or off ragged cliffs then the shepherd must continually guide them to *"the right path." "Right paths"* are the paths which are right for you and me. They represent those decisions and directions that will fulfil God's will for me. The Lord leads us specifically, personally, intimately, even down to the details of every day.

2. Righteous Paths

They represent a daily walk that is pleasing to God. God's plan for us revolves around holy living.

In an exciting revival service, people began to testify. The meeting got a little out of hand. One man stood and said: *"I've been smoking three packets of cigarettes a day - and I'm going to quit." "I've been drinking two cans of beer a day - and I'm going to quit,"* echoed another man. *"I've been cursing an awful lot - and I'm going to quit,"* confessed another. Caught up in the excitement of the moment, a little old lady stood up and said: *"I haven't been doing anything - I'm going to quit."* We can be guilty of doing things that are wrong, but we can also be guilty of not doing things that are right. One is as bad as the other. The problem with so many of us is we have 'a restoration mentality'. Yes, *"He restoreth my soul",* but He does that in order to lead me in paths of righteousness.

(3) THE PROOF OF RESTORATION

"For His name's sake."

One commonly held misconception about sheep is that they can just *"get along anywhere."* Nothing could be further from the truth! No other class of livestock requires more careful handling, more detailed direction, than do sheep. The greatest single safeguard which a shepherd has in handling his flock is to keep them on the move. They must not be left on the same pasture too long. Rather, they must be shifted from pasture to pasture. This is the secret for healthy flocks and land. Indeed, the shepherd's name and reputation depend on how effectively he keeps his flock moving onto fresh pasture. Put another way, people get some idea of the kind of man the shepherd is by the kind of sheep he has. The shepherd's name, honour, reputation – all based on the health and obedience of the sheep.

Notice what David said, *"He restoreth my soul"*:

(a) NOT FOR OUR NAMES' SAKE

It is not that a reputation for godliness may be won. It is not that a believer may be able to say to his fellow believers: *"I am holier than you."* It is not that some preacher may give the impression that he is sinlessly perfect. Why does the Lord want healthy sheep? Not for our names' sake.

(b) BUT FOR HIS NAME'S SAKE

This expression is used often in the Bible. It means for God to be glorified in the way we live. God has bound up His name with the health of His sheep. God's name, God's character, is at stake by the way you live. *Did you know the name of Jehovah is judged by the people in this place?* Are you jealous for the honour of God's name? On your job - what do people think of the name of Jesus Christ? Where you live - what do people think of the name of Jesus Christ? At your university - what do people think of the name of Jesus Christ? They are judging the name of Jesus Christ by the way you live. Do you recall what Paul says about the Jews? *"For the name of God is blasphemed among the Gentiles through you"* (Romans 2 verse 24). If I am His sheep and He is my Shepherd, I do not want to disgrace that name. The Bible says: *"A good name is rather to be chosen than great riches"* (Proverbs 22 verse 1).

Do you not tell your children when they are going out at night: *"Remember the family name! Remember who you are and whose you are!"*? I believe the Lord would say to us this: *"Remember you are*

My people, and the sheep of My pasture. My name, My honour, is linked to you and I want to lead you in paths of righteousness."

One day, towards the close of the 18th century, a man and a lady sat in a stagecoach as it rumbled its way through the English countryside. She was sitting reading the words of the hymn: *"Come, Thou Fount of every blessing"*. Suddenly, she turned to the gentleman and enquired if he knew the hymn. After a period of silence, he burst into tears: *"Madam"*, he said, *"I am the poor, unhappy man who composed that hymn many years ago and I would give a thousand worlds if I had them to enjoy the feelings that I had then."*

The man on the stagecoach was Robert Robinson. The hymn was the product of his pen some thirty years previously. Robinson had been influenced by the ministry of George Whitefield and in 1759 he became the pastor of the Baptist Church in Cambridge. The church grew, souls were saved and Robinson became well-known. However, the popularity was too much for him and he suffered a lapse in his faith. As the years passed, he faded from the scene. But now in the providence of God he was brought to the hymn he had written. One of the verses of that hymn contains the lines:

> *"Prone to wander, Lord, I feel it,*
> *Prone to leave the God I love."*

"To wander," is what Robinson did - *"to restore"* is what the Shepherd did. That day, Robert Robinson experienced the ministry of restoration.

Are you a wandering sheep? Out of fellowship with the Shepherd? Will you come to Him and say, in the closing lines of that verse:

> *"Here's my heart, O take and seal it,*
> *Seal it for Thy courts above."*

CHAPTER 4

Victory In The Valley

According to the *'Our Daily Bread'* entry for 2nd April 1994, Sarah Winchester's husband, William, had acquired a fortune by manufacturing and selling rifles. After he died of influenza in 1918, she moved to San Jose, California. Because of her grief and her long-time interest in spiritualism, Sarah sought out a medium to contact her dead husband. The medium told her: *"As long as you keep building your home, you will never face death."* Sarah believed the spiritualist, so she bought an unfinished mansion and started to expand it. It cost $5.5 million at a time when workmen earned 50 c a day. The mansion had 150 rooms, 13 bathrooms, 2,000 doors, 47 fireplaces and 10,000 windows. But the words did not work. On 5th September 1922, she died in her sleep. She left enough materials so that they could have continued building for another 80 years. Today that house stands as more than a tourist attraction. *It is a silent witness to the dread of death that holds millions of people in bondage* (Hebrews 2 verse 15).

How different is the story of the little lady who walked with God for many years. She was a saint in every measure of the word. At last her body grew frail. Life was ebbing away. She was on her death-bed. Her loved ones were around her, wringing their hands and weeping. She looked up at them and said: *"Go ahead and cry if you must, but do not cry for me"*. She explained: *"I am tickled to death to die!"*

We don't like to discuss death, but we need to learn how to deal with death. Almost every week I find myself with my grandchildren going for a walk in the graveyard in Moira Parish Church and when they ask me: *"Granda, what are these?"*, I tell them: *"Graves!*

People who die are buried here - and look there is someone who was saved. They have a Bible text on their grave." You might say: *"How awful, filling a child's mind with those kind of thoughts."* No, it's good to have those thoughts. We are not trying to scare our children, but we want them to understand the reality of life, death, and eternity. When we are caused to think of death, God uses that to bring us to realise the brevity of life and what we should be doing with our lives.

Now David had this in mind when he wrote this beautiful Psalm, especially verse 4. David spoke of a valley called *"the valley of the shadow of death."* Now there is such a valley in Israel. There is a valley called *"the valley of the shadow of death."* Many feel that a place called the **Wadi Kelt** was the specific gorge that David had in mind. It is near Bethlehem, and David probably led his sheep through the Wadi Kelt many times, taking them down to the pasture lands of the Jordan Valley during the winter and early spring months. The city of Jericho at the eastern end of the Wadi Kelt is a desert oasis and the area around it is well-watered in winter and spring. The word **"Wadi"** is a Middle Eastern term meaning *"deep valley, or ravine."* The valley parallels the old Roman road to Jericho - the backdrop of the parable of the Good Samaritan in Luke 10.

In David's day and in our Lord's Day, there was this *"valley of the shadow of death."* David would use this valley as he would take his sheep down to Jericho in the winter time and then when spring would come David would lead his sheep through that valley again to the greener pastures in the highlands of Judea.

As a shepherd, David had led his sheep through that valley and David says: *"The Lord is to me what I have been to my sheep."* David had discovered **"Victory in the Valley."**

We need to learn to do the same thing and there are three things that will help us to do that:

(1) THE FACT OF DEATH IS DECLARED

Death is a fact we must accept. Did you notice how the verse

Chapter 4

begins? "*Yea*" not "*Nay*". It is a fact we do not want to face, but the Bible says: *"It is appointed unto men once to die, but after this the judgment"* (Hebrews 9 verse 27). If the Lord Jesus does not come soon, we are all going through the door of death. Solomon said in the book of Ecclesiastes: *"To every thing there is a season, and a time to every purpose under the heaven: a time to be born, and a time to die"* (Ecclesiastes 3 verses 1 and 2). Just as surely as there is a time to be born, the Bible says there is a time to die. We cannot escape it. You see:

(a) DEATH IS ACTUAL.

"Yea!" It is a reality. We speak of statistics and a lot could be given. Here is one: One out of one die.

(b) DEATH IS INDIVIDUAL.

"Yea, though I walk." Not: *"they walk."* You know when a preacher talks about death, do you know what happens in the human mind? Your mind says: *"Yes, you tell them, preacher. Tell them about death".*

(c) DEATH IS PROBLEMATICAL.

The problem with death is that you and I do not know when we are going to die. *"Yea though I walk."* David the shepherd is walking through that valley with his sheep, but he does not know from one moment to the next what is going to happen. You see, that valley was not only *"useful"*, because it led to great feeding grounds, but it was *"dangerous"*. In some places, it is only about 12 feet wide. Even at high noon, it is always full of shadows. There are caves there and shadowy places. In Bible times, there were bears, robbers and steep places there where the sheep might fall. For David and for us, we live a step at a time. David himself said: *"There is but a step between me and death"* (1 Samuel 20 verse 3). The old man; the young mother; the little child may drop his toys to grapple with the iron strength of death. I must preach as *"never sure to preach again - a dying man to dying men"*. Do you recall James' words: *"For what is your life? It is even a vapour, that appeareth for a little time, and then vanisheth away"* (James 4 verse 14).

We count our years at each birthday, but God tells us to number our days (Psalm 90 verse 12). After all, we live a day at a time - and those days rush by quickly, the older we grow. *"It is of the Lord's mercies that we are not consumed"* (Lamentations 3 verse 22). Life is a gift from God. We should say: *"If the Lord will, we shall live, and do this, or that"* (James 4 verse 15). Do you realize that your life is passing? Have you grasped it is just like a vapour, like your breath on a frosty morning, like the steam out of the kettle? How are you spending it? Are you wasting it or investing it? Are you living that life of yours for God, for Heaven, for holiness, for souls? Are you seeking *"first the kingdom of God and His righteousness"* (Matthew 6 verse 33)?

(2) THE FIGURE OF DEATH IS DESCRIBED

David is describing death figuratively here and the figure that David uses gives us some comforting thoughts about death. He likens death to walking through a valley - where there are shadows - but where he will fear no evil for the Divine Shepherd is with him.

If we look at this figure carefully, we will notice three wonderful truths. There can be:

(a) NO VALLEY WITHOUT MOUNTAINS.

It is impossible. There can be no valley without mountains.

You see, this is *"the valley psalm"*. It lies between two mountain peaks. Psalm 22 deals with Mount Calvary. It tells of the *Crucifixion of the Messiah.* Psalm 24 deals with Mount Zion. It tells of the *Coronation of the Messiah.* So Psalm 23 is a valley between mountains. Over here are the blood-drenched slopes of Mount Calvary and over there are the sunlit peaks of Mount Zion. Here we have *Crucifixion,* over there we have *Coronation* - and we are living in the valley.

Chapter 4

Do you recall what we said about our Shepherd? The Lord Jesus is described three times in the New Testament as a Shepherd. He is the Good Shepherd – that is Mount Calvary. He is the Chief Shepherd – that is Mount Zion. But, He is also the Great Shepherd - and that's the valley experience with the One who now lives for me.

So in **Psalm 22**, we have the **Good Shepherd dying** for the sheep. In **Psalm 24**, we have the **Chief Shepherd coming** for the sheep. But, in **Psalm 23**, the **Great Shepherd**, risen from the dead, is **leading** the sheep. So do you see where we are? We are living between two mountains. We are living now in the valley of Psalm 23, where the Shepherd ministers to us.

That phrase: *"the valley of the shadow of death"* has been translated in various ways. One translation is: *"Yea, when I walk in a gloomy ravine"*. J.D. Jones described the words to mean a *"valley of deep gloom"*. Still others have translated the words as: *"the valley of deep darkness"*. I think that David was thinking not only of death but of the valley experiences through which we pass during this life, the dark hours that are often experienced as we move ***"From Earth to Glory"***. What we are talking about are real life problems. Disease and disability. Protracted legal problems. Prolonged financial pressures. Loved ones in crisis. War. Children in trouble. Marriage on the ropes. Loneliness. Addiction. Depression. Terminal illness. Old age. Dementia. Death. Are you in one of these valleys?

Catherine Booth, wife of the founder of the Salvation Army, William Booth, once wrote: *"Darkness gathers thicker than ever around the path I tread, and doubt, gloom, melancholy and despair"*. R. W. Dale was pastor of Carr's Lane in Birmingham. Someone spoke of his church as being the greatest church in the world at one time. Yet Dale wrote: *"Seasons of depression, heavy, terrible, overwhelming come over me without apparently any cause and stay in spite of means which seem most powerful to effect their removal"*. If you are in the "valley of deep darkness," your Great Shepherd can bring you through it.

There is no valley without mountains. There is also:

(b) NO SHADOW WITHOUT LIGHT.

Do you see that word *"shadow"?* This is not the valley of death. There is a <u>Death Valley</u> in California, but there is no death valley in Psalm 23. It is the valley of *"the shadow of death."*

Our Lord's final journey to the Cross was through the Wadi Kelt, the *"Way of Blood"*, the *"Bloody Pass"*. It is Matthew who traces the trip for us in Matthew 20 verses 17 to 19. He says: *"And as they departed from Jericho, a great multitude followed Him …. And when they drew nigh unto Jerusalem"* (Matthew 20 verse 29 and Matthew 21 verse 1).

The only way to travel from Jericho to Jerusalem was the Wadi Kelt, the way of blood, the valley of the shadow of death. Christ has travelled it before us – and then, on the Cross, He met the substance.

"Through death He destroyed him that had the power of death" (Hebrews 2 verse 14).

Christ *"abolished death, and hath brought life and immortality to light through the gospel"* (2 Timothy 1 verse 10).

Christ pulled the sting out of death. He took the gloom out of the grave. He has taken the dread out of dying. Now *"a shadow"* may frighten you, but it will never hurt you.

After the funeral service of his first wife, the late Donald Grey Barnhouse, the pastor of Tenth Presbyterian Church, Philadelphia was thinking about how he could convey to his children the loss of their mother. One day after the funeral service, they were down town. The father was doing some shopping and the children were in the car. They looked over on the wall of a department store and saw the shadow of a truck and the shadow was even larger than the truck because the sun was setting low in the west and it became a huge shadow on the department store wall. They said: *"Daddy, look at the big shadow of the truck"*. The father thought: *"I'll teach them a lesson"*. So he said: *"Children, if you had your choice,*

Chapter 4

would you rather be hit by the shadow or the truck?" "Oh," they said: "that is easy. We would rather be hit by that shadow of the truck than by the truck itself. The shadow cannot hurt us". Then Barnhouse, the master illustrator, said: "It was only the shadow that hit Mummy. The truck hit Jesus 2000 years ago at Calvary". A tremendous lesson, was it not?

Christ has taken the sting out of death, the gloom out of the grave, the dread out of dying. He has become our Victor. Now He fills the valley with the light and safety of His presence. Isaiah 9 verse 2 puts it like this: "They that dwell in the land of the shadow of death, upon them hath the light shined". There can be no valley without mountains and no shadow without light - and:

(c) NO EVIL WITHOUT GOOD.

"I will fear no evil." The Hebrew word for "evil" includes more than moral evil. It can be translated "distress, misery, injury, calamity and trouble". "I will fear no evil." Why? "For Thou art with me." David is comparing the evil with the great Shepherd of the sheep. Who is the "Thou"? Who does David mean? "The LORD" (verse 1). All capitals! "Jehovah" - the most sacred name the Jews had for God. Do you recall that when God charged Moses to bring His people out of bondage, Moses began to make excuses? "Who am I, that I should go?" (Exodus 3 verse 11) "They shall say to me, What is His name? What shall I say unto them? And God said unto Moses, 'I AM THAT I AM'" (verses 13 and 14).

God did not say "I was" or "I will be". He said: "I am that I am". God said: "I am" not "used to be" or "going to be". He said: "I am". The great eternal God. Tell them: "I am" sent you.

"Jehovah is My name." That name is not mentioned in the New Testament. Why not? Because Jesus Christ is our Jehovah. Jehovah .... Jesus. Do you see what David was saying? "There may be evil but Jehovah is with me, Jesus is with me."

Some years ago, a medical missionary came to the end of life's journey. He had served the Lord for many years and was dying of leukaemia. He knew how far the disease had spread and he knew how long he had to live. He wrote a letter to the assemblies with which he had associated down through the years. *"Brethren, David speaks of the valley of the shadow of death. I have now come to the valley but I find no shadows there. On the contrary, I have found that the 'path of the just is as the shining light, that shineth more and more unto the perfect day' "* (Proverbs 4 verse 18).

(3) THE FEAR OF DEATH IS DEFEATED

The word *"fear"* is found approximately 330 times throughout the Old Testament. It is most often used to speak of reverential awe produced when a person is in God's presence. (For example, Exodus 1 verse 17 and 1 Samuel 12 verse 14) However, here the Hebrew word (*"yare"*) is used to describe fear produced by the anticipation of evil. (See also Exodus 14 verse 13)

Do you fear death? Is it because you know that you face death without Christ? I recall walking into the Mater Hospital, Belfast, just minutes after Pastor Ivan Thompson got the news that he had an incurable brain tumour. In the weeks that followed I was often at his bedside. As I visited him, I watched that big frame getting weaker and weaker. *"Denis"*, he said, *"God has been good to me and I want to glorify Him in death"*. I remember the day he discussed with me his funeral arrangements. He said *"I want you to preach at the grave"* and then with that familiar twinkle in his eye he said: *"Now, here's what to preach on at the grave."*

Is it not great to *"finish well"*? Do you know how we can defeat the fear of death and get *"victory in the valley"*? By remembering three things about our sufficient Shepherd. Don't forget:

(a) THE PRESENCE OF THE SHEPHERD.

<u>He is with you.</u> Robert Morgan in his outstanding book *"The Lord is my Shepherd"* says: *"This verse is powerful in its imagery but also in its grammar. Here in the valley in the middle of the Psalm and at the most difficult moment in a sheep's life, we are awestruck by the dramatic change of the pronouns"*.

Chapter 4

Did you notice that very remarkable change in the pronoun in verse 4? You see, up until now David has been speaking of *"He"*, but now as he passes through the dark valley he gets closer to the Lord and he says: *"Thou"*. David is no longer talking **about** Him. He is talking **to** Him. To whom? Jehovah. The Ultimate is my Intimate. Think about it, we will not have to cross Jordan alone. I will not have to die alone. I will know what He meant when He said: *"I will never leave thee"* (Hebrews 13 verse 5).

John McNeill, the Scottish preacher, in his youth was a ticket clerk at a busy station. Saturday was very busy, yet no matter how late he was he always wanted to spend Sunday with his family. Home was 7 miles away along a dreary road which had a bad reputation. Early one Sunday morning, just after midnight, he set off to walk the 7 miles home. He had to pass through a section that was known as *"the valley of the shadow"*. When he came to that point, it was very dark. Trees met overhead - and his feet barely touched the ground. Then suddenly, twenty yards in front of him, there rang out a strong manly voice: *"Is that you, Johnny?"* For a moment he was startled, then he recovered. It was his father who had come out to meet him at the worst part of the road. His voice delivered him from all fears. John's night was turned to light. With his father's hand on his shoulder, his voice ringing in his ear, his footfall beside him, he feared no evil. All that made home was with him.

Are you in some *"dark valley"*? He is with you <u>now,</u> and will be with you <u>then </u>when you come to *"the valley of the shadow of death"*.

The presence of the Shepherd and:

(b) THE POWER OF THE SHEPHERD.

<u>He is for you.</u> David says: *"Thy rod and thy staff they comfort me"* *(verse 4)*. The rod was to **guard** the sheep. The staff was to **guide** the sheep. When you come to die, the Lord will be with you. There will be *His Presence:* but there will also be *His Power*. His rod will be there to protect you from all the powers of evil and His staff

will be there to draw you up close to Him as you walk *"through the valley"* and as your feet touch the chilly waters of the river of death.

But, there is a third truth to remember:

(c) THE PURPOSE OF THE SHEPHERD.

He will bring you through. What is the purpose of the Shepherd? It is **through** the valley. In Israel, the shepherd would lead his flock through that valley to greener pastures. It was always better ahead. David did not use the phrase: *"Yea, though I walk in the valley"*. No, the emphasis is on ***"through"***. This indicates a temporary state, a transition, a brighter path ahead, a hopeful future. For non-Christians, blessings are temporal and problems are eternal. For Christians, problems are always temporal and blessings always eternal.

It is not a cul-de-sac. It is *through*. Christ has "kicked the end" out of the grave. Our Shepherd will bring us through. Are you today in a *"valley of deep darkness"*? David knew enough about a shepherd to know that a shepherd would never lead the sheep through *"the valley of the shadow"* unless he was leading them to a better place.

Someone asked a man: *"What is your favourite verse in the Bible?"* He replied: *"It came to pass"*. He went on to explain: *"Whatever it is, I know it hasn't come to stay!"*

Are you in a storm? It has come to pass - and we are going through. Fanny Crosby penned those lovely words:

> *All the way my Saviour leads me,*
> *What have I to ask beside?*
> *Can I doubt His tender mercy,*
> *Who through life has been my Guide?*
> *Heavenly peace, divinest comfort,*
> *Here by faith in Him to dwell,*
> *For I know whate'er befall me,*
> *Jesus doeth all things well.*

Robert Morgan, in his book on this Psalm, tells the story of Mrs Berry, the wife of Joseph Berry, a pastor in Hackney, London, in the 1800s. Mrs. Berry was a lady who was tireless in her efforts on behalf of the poor. When she took ill, she turned to Psalm 23 and found it *"a heavenly message for me."* She told her husband: *"If there must be a funeral sermon, let it be Psalm 23 verse 4".* As her health continued to fail, she had smatterings of conversation with her loved ones, saying: *"Almost at home. My precious Bible, I never thought it could have supported me thus, but it does. I have not an anxious wish. It is Heaven already begun. I am as happy as I can be on this side of Heaven. Jesus is very precious. I have no anxiety".*

Still later, she whispered to a friend: *"It is so sweet to die in Jesus. Bless God, my dear, I am so happy though I walk through the valley".* Then in her final moments, her friends caught a few words from her dying lips, evidently inspired by Psalm 23: *"Valley .... Shadow .... Home .... Jesus .... Peace."* And with that she went to Heaven.

She had ***"Victory in the Valley".*** We can have too, if we remember He is with us, He is for us, and He will see us through. ***His Presence is Dear; His Power is Near; His Purpose is clear.*** Your Sufficient Shepherd will see you through.

CHAPTER 5

How Good Is The God We Adore

The story is told of two men who went to the same church one Sunday morning. One heard the organist miss a note and winced. He saw a teenager talking when everyone was supposed to *"bow in prayer"*. He felt the deacon was watching what he put in the offering plate and it aggravated him. He caught the preacher making a slip of the tongue five times in the sermon, and as he walked out he said to himself: *"What good does it do me to come to church?"*

The other man heard the organist play an arrangement of *"A Mighty Fortress is our God"* and was thrilled by it. He was moved by a young person who gave their testimony. He was glad when they received an offering for missions. He especially appreciated the sermon for it answered a question he had been bothered about for a long time. As he left the service that day, he said to himself: *"How can anyone come here and not feel the presence of the Lord?"*

Both men went to the same church. They attended the same service. They found what they were looking for! There are some who see only the negative. There are others who see the positive.

Here is David looking back over the days of his life. He says: **"How good is the God we adore!"** David thought of God positively.

Do you know what the devil wants you to do in relation to your life? He wants you to think negatively about God. He wants you not to have good feelings. The devil knows that if he can get you thinking negatively about God, he can do almost anything with

Chapter 5

you. Do you recall what he did in the Garden of Eden? When he appeared as a serpent to Eve? He asked her a question: *"Hath God said, Ye shall not eat of every tree of the garden?"* (Genesis 3 verse 1). God had not said that. God had said: *"Of every tree of the garden thou mayest freely eat"* (Genesis 2 verse 16). With the exception of one tree, God had said, in effect: **"Help yourself!"** But, do you see what the devil did? He tried to get Eve to think negatively about God - and he is still doing that job today. People today think of God as some kind of cosmic killjoy. People just think negatively about God. When they think of serving God, they think of it as something they have to do in order to get to Heaven - not as something they want to do.

What a distorted idea about the goodness of our God! When we consider verse 5 of this Psalm, we see: **"<u>How good is the God we adore!</u>"**

Some have suggested that David changed metaphors in verse 5, so we have in verses 1 to 4 *"The Shepherd and the Sheep"* and then in verses 5 and 6 *"The Host and the Guests"*. We have here:

1. <u>A Prepared Table.</u>

"Thou preparest a table." The word *"table"* could mean flat table areas where the sheep could graze easily. A perfect place for summer grazing. *"Thou preparest."* That means God Himself sets the table! To "set a table" is to honour the person who is coming. David is saying: *"God has put on an apron. Jehovah has prepared a table for me. He loves me. He welcomes me. I am special to Him."*

2. <u>An Anointed Head.</u>

In a wealthy home in the Middle East, there would be a cruise of oil by the door. Very expensive and perfumed. It would be there for special occasions. When a very important guest would come into the home - maybe a family member who had been gone for a long time or someone dearly loved - the host would come and greet his friend. There would be a kiss on either cheek and then he would reach into the bowl of ointment and he would put that ointment on the face, hair and head of his guest. It would perfume that person and refresh him. They called that: *"the anointing of the head"*. Throughout the rest of the feast that person would smell the sweet perfume that was on his head. It would make him feel good. They do something like this in Hawaii. When you go into a home, they take a ring of flowers called a *"Lay"* and they put it around your neck. The whole time you are there, you are smelling those flowers. It is their way of saying: *"You are welcome. You are special"*.

This was for a special occasion. Do you recall that woman in Luke 7 who was a sinner, taking and breaking that alabaster box of ointment? She anointed the feet of Christ. Simon complained and the Lord Jesus said: *"My head with oil thou didst not anoint"*. That is: *"Simon, you did not show Me that reverence and respect. This woman has not only anointed My head but My feet with this perfume."* This anointing was to refresh. It was saying: *"You are special!"*

3. The Overflowing Cup.

"My cup runneth over." In Bible times, they did not have the hotels that we have today. There were a few inns, but most of them were dirty, filthy, crowded, expensive and some very immoral. But there was a law in the land. It was called *"the law of hospitality"*. If you were travelling and you came to a man's house in the middle of the day and you asked for food, it would be unthinkable that he would let you go without first feeding you. It was just the law of the land that a stranger would be taken in and given a meal. Now, suppose you had done your duty. You have fed him, been respectful towards him. It is time for him to go. But maybe you have come to like him and you want him to stay. Here is the way you would do it.

The host would take the guest's empty cup at the end of the meal and the host would take the pitcher and, if it was time for this man to go, he would fill that cup half-full. Do you know what that meant? *"When you have finished your desert, hit the road."* He would not have to say a word! But if the host would come with that pitcher and begin to pour into that cup and fill it up to the brim and then just let it overflow - do you know what that meant? *"You are special. I love you and you are invited to stay in my home overnight. You are my special guest."*

Do you now see what David is saying? *"Look, Jehovah has prepared a table for me. I am special. He has anointed my head. He loves me. My cup runs over. He is showing hospitality to me. He is saying to me that I am His friend".*

Who is our Jehovah? The Lord Jesus. Do you recall what Christ said: *"Ye are My friends"* (John 15 verse 15). You do not think negatively about a friend. What is a friend? A friend is *"someone who knows all about you and loves you just the same"*. A friend is *"someone who comes in when all the world walks out"*. Do you see what David is saying? *"The Lord is a friend." "What a friend we have in Jesus!"* He prepares a table. He anoints my head. My cup runs over.

Do not ever let the devil get you to think negatively about God. For *"How good is the God we adore"*. Indeed, God's goodness is seen in these three expressions.

Notice for example:

(1) WHAT THE SHEPHERD PREPARES FOR US.

That is His Work: *"Thou preparest."* William Avery Rogers in his book: *"The Shepherd and His Sheep"* spoke about the four perils that sheep face. The peril of **Exhaustion:** the danger of losing their strength and becoming exhausted. The peril of **Environment:** there were extreme temperatures such as the heat during the day and the cold at night. There was the rough terrain and sudden storms. There was the peril of **Entanglement:** a sheep could get caught by its heavy wool in a thorn bush. There was the peril of **Enemies:** the dangerous weeds, the wild beasts and the poisonous snakes. Though it was tedious and tiring, the shepherd would prepare a *"table in the presence of their enemies"*. It requires a lot of hard work to convert plateaus into pastures. These tablelands do not just appear on the horizon fully developed. They must be prepared and this groundwork takes years, even generations.

A missionary was visiting in a hospital speaking to the patients about Christ. She came to an underdeveloped little boy whose tiny form drew out her deepest sympathy. When she talked to him at first he showed little interest, but he became more interested. Prayerfully and carefully, she told him of our wonderful Saviour. She made several calls with him but he was unwilling to make any commitment. One morning, however, she found him beaming: "*What has happened?*" she asked. "*Oh*", he replied, "*I always knew that Jesus was necessary, but I never knew until yesterday that Jesus was enough*".

The Lord Jesus meets the deepest hungers of our heart and satisfies the deepest longings of our soul. "*Thou preparest.*" Do you ever think about the feasts, meals, tables that our Lord prepared for the disciples? For example, the Shepherd prepares:

(a) THE TABLE OF REPLENISHMENT.

The Lord fed the five-thousand (Luke 9 verse 12). He performed a miracle to do it with five loaves and two fishes. He prepared a table of replenishment when there was the enemy of inadequacy. Has He ever done that for you? We can feel so inadequate. We can run out of resources. Then the Lord prepares a table before us. We need it, but we do not deserve it. Was there any way that you could explain the feeding of the five-thousand? *Not any way except God.* What is there about your life that cannot be explained apart from God? If your neighbour can explain you, then you are just like him, only religious - and that is not going to convince him. But when he sees a God who is supernaturally meeting your needs and preparing for you a table of replenishment then you are going to be believable.

(b) THE TABLE OF RESTORATION.

Do you recall when Simon Peter denied Christ in Luke 22? The Saviour was crucified and then raised from the dead. The disciples were discouraged, half-believing and half-doubting and Peter

Chapter 5

said: *"I go a fishing"* (John 21 verse 3). They fished all night and caught nothing. Then the Master said: *"Children, have ye any meat?"* He directed them to a multitude of fish and when they came to land - what had the Saviour done? He had a table prepared. There was fish on the hot coals and fresh bread.

Now we can understand the fish being there. This was beside the Sea of Galilee - but from where did Christ get that bread? Had He turned stones into bread? Had He said to Satan: *"I will do it when I want to - not when you want Me to"*?

Can you imagine fishing all night and catching nothing? Here they were - seven big, hungry, disillusioned fishermen and the Risen Lord said: *"Come and dine."* Have you failed the Saviour? Have you, like Peter, denied Christ, even with oaths and curses? Dear failing friend, there is a table of restoration for you and He says to you: *"Come and dine"*.

(c) THE TABLE OF REMEMBRANCE.

Before He was crucified, the Lord Jesus kept the Passover feast. Luke 22 verse 14 declares: *"When the hour was come, He sat down, and the twelve apostles with Him."*

He was the Host at the table and He said: *"This do in remembrance of Me"*. Do we fully appreciate what it has cost Him to prepare this table for us? Bless God, we can sit down at the table He has prepared for us. Do you avail yourself of that privilege? Do you take seriously the command of Christ: *"This do in remembrance of Me"*? Are you obedient to that command?

Then there is a wonderful table yet to come:

(d) THE TABLE OF REJOICING.

Christ said: *"I will not drink henceforth of this fruit of the vine, until that day when I drink it new with you in My Father's kingdom"* (Matthew 26 verse 29). Our Lord who is preparing a place is also preparing a feast and one of these days we are going to sit down with Him in the marriage supper of the Lamb (Revelation 19 verse 9). One of these days we are going to sit down at that table.

"How good is the God we adore." Do not think negatively about God. When the Bible describes our salvation, it does not describe it as a funeral, but as a feast!

(2) WHAT THE SHEPHERD PURPOSES FOR US

That is His Watchfulness: *"Thou anointest."* The sheep may be on the high ridges, where there are clear springs, where the grass is fresh and tender, where there is intimate contact with the shepherd. Suddenly, however, we find *"a fly in the ointment"*. In the terminology of the shepherd: *"Summer time is fly time"*. Sheep are especially troubled by the nose fly. They work their way up the nasal passages into the sheep's head. They burrow into the flesh and there set up an intense irritation accompanied by severe inflammation. Did you ever see sheep deliberately beating their heads against trees, rocks or posts? They are seeking relief from the nose fly, and only the diligent attention of the shepherd can forestall the problems of *"fly time."* In this action by the shepherd we see:

(a) THE HURTS THE SHEPHERD ATTENDS.

When the sheep entered the fold one by one, the shepherd would *count* them, then he would *call* them and then he would *caress* them. He would be looking not only for the flies, but for the cuts, the wounds, the sores, the bruises, the eyes that are inflamed by dust or sunshine. The shepherd is aware. He is alert. He is awake to all that is happening.

In our journey of life, there are many ways in which we can get hurt, and there are many folk who will hurt us.

Life has many ways of bruising and wounding us.

Sometimes life itself can leave us weary and sick in heart. Does our Divine Shepherd ignore these hurts? Does He pay no attention

Chapter 5

to the scratches, wounds, hurts and ailments of us, His sheep? Absolutely not!

> *Amid the trials that I meet*
> *Amid the thorns that pierce my feet,*
> *One thought remains supremely sweet,*
> *Thou thinkest Lord of me.*

In the burdens of life, He knows, He cares and He understands.

> *Are your crosses too heavy to carry,*
> *And burdens too heavy to bear;*
> *Are there heartaches and tears and anguish*
> *And there's no one who seems to care?*
>
> *Standing somewhere in the shadows, you'll find Jesus,*
> *He's the Friend who always cares and understands,*
> *Standing somewhere in the shadows, you will find Him,*
> *And you'll know Him by the nail prints in His hands.*
>
> *Are there shadows of deep disappointment*
> *And trusts that have proven untrue;*
> *Has the darkness of night settled round you,*
> *Has your hope and your faith wavered too?*
>
> *Has the storm over-shadowed your sunshine,*
> *And life lost attraction for you;*
> *Have the dreams that you cherished been broken*
> *Is your soul filled with bitterness too?*

(b) THE HEALING THE SHEPHERD APPLIES.

"Thou anointest my head with oil." The shepherd always carried with him a bottle of oil. At the first sign of flies, he would apply an antidote to their heads. When he found one of his sheep with a scratch, he would pour oil over it. If there was a wound, he would rub in the oil. If the sheep had suffered from the heat, he would rub its head down with oil. *The oil had medicinal qualities that would*

speed healing and prevent infection. Thank God for the oil of the Holy Spirit who in His varied ministries brings restoration, comfort, joy and peace (Isaiah 61 verse 3).

Helen Kehn was the youngest of five children and had never known what it was to be alone. Her family always did things together. But there came a day when she found herself alone. Her parents died first and then her brother. Two of her sisters died exactly one month apart and the last of her three sisters had just died.

One of the things she dreaded was going back to an empty house. Previously, she didn't even have a key to the house. There had always been someone there to let her in. She was returning home and no-one would be there. She drove the car into the garage and sat there for a while, working up the courage to walk into the empty house alone. As she walked up the path, she prayed: "O God, help me". As soon as she walked into the house, she turned the radio on just so there would be sound in those empty rooms. As she hung up her coat she caught the words that were coming from the radio,

> *No, never alone, no, never alone,*
> *He promised never to leave me,*
> *Never to leave me alone.*

It was the *"Old Fashioned Revival Hour Quartet"* singing, but it was more than a quartet singing. It was the voice of God, speaking to her heart. Standing there, she realized that she would never be alone. That day the Lord anointed her hurt with His oil! The Lord has oil for your hurts. You are His child and He knows you and all that is going on in your life. He knows just what you need and with David you can say: *"Thou anointest my head with oil"*.

(3) WHAT THE SHEPHERD PROVIDES FOR US

That is His Wealth: *"My cup runneth over."* (verse 5) Providing water for the sheep required a lot of hard work, especially on the tablelands away from natural rivers and ponds. A mature sheep needs between one and three gallons of water each day.

Shepherds had to dig wells. Those wells had to be maintained and a stone fitted for the covering. The sheep did not really appreciate all the work that went into it but they were satisfied when their water troughs overflowed. Here David was thinking of how good God had been to him and all the blessings he had experienced in his life.

There was:

(a) THE OVERFLOW OF GOD'S BLESSINGS.

"My cup runneth over." Why? Because Christ drained His cup (Matthew 26 verse 39), ours can overflow. All our blessings in this life and the next were purchased by the Good Shepherd when He laid down His life for His sheep. Christ said: *"I am come that they might have life, and that they might have it more abundantly"* (John 10 verse 10). Think about it – our cup runs over. He speaks of life, but not just of life: *"life more abundant"*. He speaks of joy, but not just of joy but *"joy unspeakable and full of glory"* (1 Peter 1 verse 8). He speaks of grace but not just of grace but *"grace sufficient"* (2 Corinthians 12 verse 9). The Lord is not talking about **necessities** but **luxuries**.

In the words of Annie Johnson Flint:

> *He giveth more grace when the burdens grow greater,*
> *He sendeth more strength when the labours increase;*
> *To added affliction, He addeth His mercy*
> *To multiplied trials, His multiplied peace.*
>
> *When we have exhausted our strength of endurance,*
> *When our strength has failed ere the day is half done,*
> *When we reach the end of our hoarded resources*
> *Our Father's full giving is only begun.*
>
> *Fear not that thy need shall exceed His provision,*
> *Our God ever yearns His resources to share;*
> *Lean hard on the arm everlasting, availing;*
> *The Father both thee and thy load will upbear.*

His love has no limit, His grace has no measure,
His power no boundary known unto men;
For out of His infinite riches in Jesus,
He giveth, and giveth, and giveth again.

Have you ever thought about God like that? As the Giving God. As the God of the open heart and the God of the open hand. God does not measure His blessings drop by drop. *"Our cup runs over."*

Then there is:

(b) THE OUTFLOW OF GOD'S BLESSINGS.

"My cup runneth over." It flows over - the question is, does it flow out? Does it flow out to others? The Bible says: *"Freely ye have received, freely give"* (Matthew 10 verse 8). Do you know what some people do? When God gives and when their cup overflows, they do not let it run over to others. Instead, they get a bigger cup.

Recall the rich farmer: *"I will pull down my barns and build greater"* (Luke 12 verse 13). *"I don't want it to run over. I don't want it to bless anyone else. I want it all for me. All for me!"* No! No! Freely he had received, freely he needed to give. Let the cup run over and be a channel of blessing to someone else.

CHAPTER 6

It Is Good Now, But It Is Better Up Ahead

Two men were traveling together on an aeroplane. One was taking a nap and the other was busy working on a crossword puzzle. He nudged his napping friend and asked: *"What is a word with three letters, with the letter 'O' in the middle, meaning, man's best friend?"* His friend mumbled: *"Dog"*. But *"dog"* did not fit. He worked at the puzzle a little longer and then said: *"The last letter is D"*. Even with the two letters *"OD"* in a three letter word describing man's best friend, they never did think of the first letter as being *"G"*.

Our quest in this book has been to find out how we can face all the days of our life. The 23rd Psalm has been our source for finding the answer. As we come to the final words and verse of the Psalm, we end up where we started, with the Lord. David has given us several secrets to facing all the days our life and they all find their source in a three letter word that means man's best friend and that word is **God.** Are you not glad that you do not have to face life without the Lord? That you can say with the hymn writer:

> *I've found a friend who is all to me.*
> *His love is ever true;*
> *I love to tell how He lifted me,*
> *And what His grace can do for you.*
>
> *Saved by His pow'r divine,*
> *Saved to new life sublime!*
> *Life now is sweet and my joy is complete,*
> *For I'm saved, saved, saved!*

He saves me from every sin and harm,
Secures my soul each day;
I'm leaning strong on His mighty arm;
I know He'll guide me all the way.

As David comes to the end of this Psalm, he is thinking about the days *behind him*, the days *before him*, and the days *beyond him*. As he does so, we can imagine him looking up toward Heaven and saying: *"Hallelujah! What a Shepherd!"*

As we finish our study of this Psalm, we are coming to that last reality before us, our Father's House. For David's actual flocks in Biblical times the trail spiralled back to Bethlehem as they returned to the family farm at the end of their seasonal migrations. For believers our trail spirals upwards as we arrive at our Father's House at the end of our earthly road. For the Christian: *"It is Good Now, but it is Better Up Ahead"*.

Satan has no happy old people. Satan has some happy young people - the kids who are living high. They have a certain amount of fun that might be called happiness, but Satan has no happy old folk. Satan always gives the best first and the worst last. The book of Proverbs says: *"Bread of deceit is sweet to a man; but afterwards his mouth shall be filled with gravel"* (Proverbs 20 verse 17).

With Satan, it always seems to start sweet, but it does not end that way. Satan is a deceiver. He is guilty of false advertising. Satan does not show the drunkard in the gutter covered with flies. He does not show the carnage on the road. He does not show the blasted lives and ruined homes. Satan always gives the best first and the worst last. But, the Lord Jesus gives the best last. Do you recall at the wedding feast – in John 2 - when the Saviour turned the water into wine? The master of ceremonies came out and said: *"I don't understand this, most give the best first but you have saved the best to the last"*.

That is what the Saviour always does. With Christ it keeps getting better and better. *"Every day with Jesus is sweeter than the day before!"*

Chapter 6

Now, that does not mean that it is not good now, but it does mean that it gets better. Is this not what David is saying? He is saying:

"It is good now".
"Surely goodness." It is good now.
"And I will dwell in the house of the LORD for ever." It is better up ahead.

Here are three thoughts that will bless your soul:

(1) BEHIND US: A HELP THAT IS SURE

As David looks behind him, he sees that there have been a couple of very special companions that have accompanied him all the days of his life. Throughout the Psalm, he has portrayed the shepherd as always being in *front* of his flock. He has always been leading the sheep, never driving them, thus always in front. But now, his reflection makes him aware that *"goodness and mercy"* have been behind him every day of all his days.

Guy King likens *"Goodness"* and *"Mercy"* to sheepdogs. He wrote: *"He (The Lord) is in front, and the sheepdogs behind, and we, His sheep, are happily sandwiched in between"*.

Do you see the word *"surely"*? It can also be translated: *"Only goodness and mercy"*. But, the best rendering seems to be: *"Surely"*. It has the basic meaning of: *"No doubt; this is absolutely true; this can never be doubted; it can never fail"*. Now look at the word *"follow"*. It is usually translated: *"pursued, chased or hunted"* (See, for example, 1 Samuel 26 verse 20)

The words of R.L. Moyer are lovely: *"Thirty-two years ago, when the writer was saved, God said to those two servants named Goodness and Mercy, 'Get on his trail. Never let him out of your sight. Pursue him to glory'"*.

Behind us there is a help that is sure. This help:

(a) IS PROVIDENTIAL.

"Goodness" is almost too big a Biblical term to describe. Robert Morgan says: *"The Hebrew word David used refers to goodness in its broadest sense, covering physical, moral, practical, economic, spiritual, emotional and eternal grace toward us in all its dimensions"*. The word *"good"* is a characteristic of God and it refers to the essential nature of His perfections and benevolence. Our God is a good God and He continually fills our lives with goodness and good things. The Lord Jesus referred to Himself as the *"Good Shepherd"* who gives His life for the sheep.

If we open the Bible anywhere we will see the goodness of God somewhere.

The Psalmist says: *"Thou art good, and doest good"* (Psalm 119 verse 68)

The Psalmist says: *"Oh how great is Thy goodness, which Thou hast laid up for them that fear thee"* (Psalm 31 verse 19).

When David looks back and sees that *"goodness"* has followed him all the days of his life, he is saying what the New Testament promises: *"And we know that all things work together for good to them that love God, to them who are the called according to His purpose"* (Romans 8 verse 28).

When David looks back, he see black days as well as bright. He sees days that were delightful, but also days that were distressful. There have been many things that were disappointing, discouraging and difficult. There had been many of those *"valley"* experiences. Yet, as David reflects on these days, he realizes that everything that had happened had been for his good. Life had been a mixture of events and happenings, yet they all had worked together for his good.

A little boy told his grandmother how *"everything"* was going wrong. Meanwhile, his grandmother was baking a cake. She asked: *"Would you like to have a snack?" "Yes!"* was his quick reply. *" Here"*, said the grandmother, *"Have some cooking oil"*. *"Yuck!"* said the little boy. *"How about a couple of raw eggs?"* asked the grandmother. *"Would you like some flour? Or baking soda?" "Grandma"*, said the little boy, *"all those things are yucky"*. The grandmother then replied: *"Yes, all those things seem bad by themselves, but when they are put together, in the right way, they make a wonderfully delicious cake"*. She went on to explain how God takes the bad things in life and turns them into something good for us.

Is this not your testimony? As we look back we see that *"goodness"* has followed us all the days of our life. Our Lord has been in control of all that has happened. Even though at the time His face was hidden, now we see His handprint on it all. Nothing, absolutely nothing, has happened in our life that first was not filtered through God's love and plan for our life. He is in control of all things. Goodness has followed us all the days of our life. It may take several days, even years, to see it, but we all can look back and see how all things have worked together for our good. Then, this help:

(b) IS VITAL.

Now if *"goodness"* represents all the Lord bestows on us that we do not deserve, then *"mercy"* represents all that He withholds that we do deserve. The Hebrew word here (*'Chesed'*) is difficult to translate but terms such as: *"Steadfast love, mercy, grace, loving kindness, faithfulness, unfailing love"* are aimed in the right direction. Where would we or David have been but for the mercy of God? Even though he was a man after God's own heart, he had not lived a blameless life. There were some dark and dirty stains on his past. Yet, as he looks back he sees that *"mercy"* has followed him all the days of his life. When he failed God, did the Lord cast him off and away? Did the Lord ever look down at him and say: *"Oh, rebellious, straying lamb. You can no longer be a part of My flock"*. When David wandered, did God leave him and turn His back on him? No! Ten thousand times, No! Instead, he had found *"mercy"*.

No doubt he had prayed many times the prayer of Psalm 51 verse 1: *"Have mercy upon me, O God"* and God had. Do you not wish that you could undo many things in the past? Especially, your sins and failures. All of us live with certain regrets. That deed once done that can never be undone; that word spoken that can never be unsaid; that opportunity missed that can never be reclaimed. When we look at the many times we sin and fail the Lord, yet realise that He still leads us, cares for us, protects and provides for us, and loves us as much as any sheep in His flock, we have to say *"mercy"* has followed us all the days of our life.

Do you see this? Behind you is a Help that is Sure: and this help is providential and vital. This help also:

(c) IS CONTINUAL.

How long will *"goodness and mercy"* follow us? They will follow us all the days of our life. No exclusions, no exceptions, no exemptions. God's sheepdogs never take a day off and they remain awake every night. *"Goodness and mercy"* shall follow us all the days of our life. Every day of all our days, they will be following us.

When Dr. Harry Ironside was pastor of Moody Memorial Church in Chicago, he had a poor old lady who lived by herself who was just haunted by fear. She had a phobia. She believed that there were two men who followed her just wherever she went. She came to see the pastor about this, she was so worried. *"Pastor"*, she said, *"I have a problem"*. He asked: *"What is it?"* She said: *"Well, everywhere I go, two men follow me. When I go the supermarket, they follow me. When I get on the tram, they follow me. When I come home, there they are behind me, constantly following me"*. He said: *"Have you told the police?"* She said: *"Yes, but they say they are not there. I know they are there. They are always there"*. Dr. Ironside said: *"You are a most blessed woman. You are a privileged woman. Do you not know who these two men are?"* She said: *"No, do you know?"* *"Oh, yes"*, he said, *"they are David's friends"*. He turned to Psalm 23 and he read these words: *"Surely goodness and mercy shall follow me all the days of my life"*. He said: *"Those two men - one is named 'goodness' and the other is named 'mercy' and God has sent them to follow you all the days of your life"*. She said: *" Pastor, that is wonderful - and to think that all this time I have been afraid of them"*. She was so happy. Every day when she would go on the streetcar, she would wait for "goodness" and "mercy" to get on. When she would come home to her apartment, she would open the door and let "goodness" and "mercy" go in. She lived the rest of her life, until she stepped over unto the other side, in perfect happiness and no more fear. You say: *"Was the pastor right to tell her that?"* Well, all of us need to understand that in a very real way *"goodness and mercy"*, God's goodness in the good times and God's mercy in the bad times, God's provision for our need and God's provision for our failure, have followed us all the days of our life.

(2) BEFORE US: A HOME THAT IS SAFE

William Avery Rogers describes how each year in the Holy Land there came a time when the weather conditions hindered the shepherd and sheep from staying out on the open range and in the temporary fold. When this time came, the shepherd turned his sheep toward his own home where he had made for them a more permanent place. He also describes how the sheep would know they were home. They would jump about and swish their tails with joy.

The phrase *"the house of the Lord"* occurs many times in the Old Testament. (See, for example, Psalm 27 verse 4; Psalm 92 verses 12 and 13 and Psalm 122 verse 1.) It referred to the Tabernacle and later to the Temple. It is the place where God's presence is centred. (See: Exodus 25 verses 9 and 22.) But when David says: *"I will dwell in the house of the Lord for ever"*, he was thinking of Heaven, where *"The tabernacle (or house) of God is with men, and He will dwell with them, and they shall be His people, and God Himself shall be with them, and be their God"* (Revelation 21 verse 3).

One of the sweetest passages in the Bible is John 14 where the Lord Jesus underscored what David said in Psalm 23: *"Let not your heart be troubled"*. He is talking about the same place as David. *"My Father's house."* The Lord would not let the hope of Heaven beat within the human bosom if it were simply a lie, a superstition, or a fond delusion. *"If it were not so, I would have told you. I go to prepare a place for you"*. The Greek word for "place" is *"topos"*, from which we get the term "topography", the study of a particular locality. Did you know that Heaven is a real place? It is not a state of mind or condition. It is a real place. It is just as real as any city on earth. It is a place so real that Christ is there in a literal, resurrected body. Heaven is a place on God's map. The Bible almost universally represents it as *"being up"*. The Psalmist said: *"If I ascend up into Heaven, Thou art there"* (Psalm 139 verse 8). The Lord Jesus said: *"No man hath ascended up into Heaven"* (John 3 verse 13). Paul talked about this place. He called it "the third heaven". He says in 2 Corinthians 12 verse 2: *"I knew a man in Christ above fourteen years ago, (whether in the body, I cannot tell; or whether out of the body, I cannot tell: God knoweth;) such an one caught up to the third heaven"*. Paul says you go there in a body or out of a body. The Lord is there in a body. Some folk are there out of a body. They will have a body later on, but he says this person was caught up to the third heaven. So there are three heavens: There is:

The Heaven of the Birds: The AERIAL Heaven
The Bible speaks of the *"fowls of heaven"* (Job 35 verse 11). They fly in the air - so that is the first heaven. The envelope of air that surrounds the earth.

The Heaven of the Stars: The STELLAR Heaven:
Do you recall God's Word to Abram: *"Look now toward heaven, and tell the number of the stars, if thou be able to number them"* (Genesis 15 verse 5). Yes, there is *"the starry heaven"*.

The Heaven of the Angels: The ETERNAL Heaven:
The very abode of God. Solomon prayed: *"Hear Thou in heaven, Thy dwelling place"* (1 Kings 8 verse 30). Someone has beautifully said: *"We see the first heaven by day, the second heaven by night and the third heaven by faith"*.

A father went off to war. His little son was afraid of what he would have to face so he wrote him a note: *"Dear Daddy, I love you and I hope you live all your life"*. We all want to live all our life, but the days of your life will come to an end and then immediately if we are Christ's we are going to step into Heaven. Yes, one day, the

"Chief Shepherd" will bring His sheep home. What a glorious day that will be! What kind of home will it be?

Well, this home called Heaven is:

(a) A PRECIOUS HOME.

David called it: *"the house of the Lord"*. Christ called it: *"My Father's house"*. The thoughts of a house or home bring to mind several things. Home is a place of retirement after a hard day's work. Home is the place where we seek escape from the strife and turmoil of the world in which we live. It is the place where we find rest and enjoy time with our loved ones. Home is home because the one we love best is there, and Heaven is home because Christ is there.

The greatest attraction in glory will not be its pearly gates, its golden streets or its chorus of angels. It will be Christ. One moment after you die, will you wake up in Heaven? In the Father's House? At home with the Lord?

(b) A PERFECT HOME

Think of the *"no mores"* there will be in Heaven. No more sea, death, sorrow, crying, pain, or sin (Revelation 21 verse 4). Now, sometimes, people ask: *"Well, what is Heaven going to be like? Will we sleep and eat? How old will we be? What will we do?"* You know the questions - I do not know the answers, but that does not bother me. The Bible says: *"It doth not yet appear what we shall be"* (1 John 3 verse 2). What is Heaven going to be like? It is going to mean the presence of all that is good and the absence of all that is evil. If that does not satisfy you - let me give you this: *It is going to be all that the loving heart of God can conceive and the omnipotent hand of God can prepare.*

(3) BEYOND US: A HOPE THAT IS SWEET

Do you see how David commences this Psalm? With the **LORD**. Do you see how David concludes this Psalm? With the **LORD**. He is our hope. We are assured of future glory and blessing because of Christ.

A little boy had been promised a new puppy for his sixth birthday. He was taken to the local pound and there were so many dogs and puppies that he had a hard time choosing which one he wanted. Finally, he picked one of the shaggiest pups, standing there wagging his tail furiously. His mother asked him: *"Why that one?"* He replied: *"I want the one with the happy ending!"*

"The house of the Lord" does not only mean *"a building of God"*, as described in 2 Corinthians 5 verse 1. We have that, of course, but this word *"house"* refers to the family or flock of the Good Shepherd.

Do you know what makes our hope so sweet?

(a) THE SHEEP WILL BE THERE.

People often ask: *"Shall we know one another in Heaven?"* George Whitefield replied: *"Shall we be greater fools than we are here?"* Of course we shall know one another in Heaven. Do you recall the story of David's baby? That child who was sick and subsequently died. Do you recall David's words? *"I shall go to him, but he shall not return to me"* (2 Samuel 12 verse 23). Is that not wonderful? *"I shall go to him."* Do you have a little baby in Heaven? Have you a father or mother who has stepped over to the other side? You are going to see them again. On the Mount of Transfiguration when Moses and Elijah appeared with the Lord Jesus in Matthew 17 verse 1, the disciples did not need to be introduced to them. They knew them and they recognised them.

Heaven is a real place. Real people are going to be there and we will know our loved ones when we get there. Oh, Moses will be there. Will it not be wonderful to talk to Moses about the tabernacle? David will be there and we will say: *"David, will you sing the 23rd Psalm for us?"* Paul will be there. How would you like to sit at his feet and have him teach you the Book of Romans and talk about our grand redemption? John the aged will be there and he will show us the mysteries of the book of Revelation. And what about old Simon Peter? He will be there and he will say: *"Did I not tell you that it would be joy unspeakable and full of glory?"*

(b) THE SHEPHERD WILL BE THERE.

What is it that makes Heaven, Heaven? *"I will dwell in the house of the Lord for ever"* or, as the Amplified Old Testament puts it: *"I will dwell in the presence of the Lord for ever"*. It is the idea of an ever-present Shepherd on the scene. That is what Paul meant when he said: *"I am willing to be absent from the body, and to be present with the Lord"* (2 Corinthians 5 verse 8). That is what Isaiah meant when he said: *"Thine eyes shall see the King in His beauty"* (Isaiah 33 verse 17). The Lord Jesus prayed: *"Father, I will that they also, whom Thou hast given Me, be with Me where I am; that they may behold My glory"* (John 17 verse 24).

> *Father of Jesus, love's reward!*
> *What rapture will it be,*
> *Prostrate before Thy throne to lie,*
> *And gaze and gaze on Thee.*

It is Good Now but it is Better Up Ahead.

Is this your prospect? The book of Jude, which forms the hallway for the Revelation of Jesus Christ, speaks about people: *"to whom is reserved the blackness of darkness for ever"*.

Are you headed toward *"the house of the Lord for ever"* or are you headed toward *"the blackness of darkness for ever"*?

Can you say: *"The Lord is my Shepherd"* and: *"And I will dwell in the house of the Lord for ever"*?

A little girl was listening to the Christmas story. When it was over she thought for a little while. Then she enquired: *"Mummy, did the baby Jesus live happily ever after?"* Subsequent to Calvary, Christ did - and in eternity He will live happily with us, His own.

> *Safe to the land! Safe to the land!*
> *The end is this;*
> *And then with Him go hand in hand*
> *Far into bliss.*

Chapter 6

From Earth to Glory

From Earth to Glory